THE OFFICIAL'S GUIDE

SOCCER

'99-00

by Carl P. Schwartz, *Referee* Associate Editor

REFEREE ENTERPRISES, INC., FRANKSVILLE, WIS.

Acknowledgment
This book is intended to supplement the rulebooks and casebooks published by the National Federation of State High School Associations (NFHS), the National Collegiate Athletic Association (NCAA) as well as the *Laws of the Game* as published by the United States Soccer Federation (USSF) and used throughout international soccer.

Referee wants to thank the NFHS, NCAA and USSF for their invaluable assistance providing interpretations, advice and guidance, which appear in this book.

The Official's Guide — Soccer '99-00 by Carl P. Schwartz, Associate Editor, *Referee* Magazine

Copyright © 1999 by Referee Enterprises, Inc., P.O. Box 161, Franksville, Wis. 53126.

Layout by Lisa Martin

Printed in the United States of America.

ISBN 1-58208-011-9

Table of Contents

Introduction

You're not getting older, you're getting better. Your decision to read this book means that you are interested in improving your officiating. With new rule changes each year, it's important to stay abreast. *Referee* adds several caseplays to help bring the rules to life in situations you are likely to face on the field.

There are some changes within each of the three major codes that govern soccer in this country, but there is some good news. The changes that effect the play of the game are minor. Moreover, the codes are getting closer to each other in their wording and interpretation.

We have a quiz, with a twist. Richard Arnold, a National Referee from Wyoming, guides us on a journey that has you taking a quiz and learning the correct answer in all three codes of law. Arnold then explains the mechanics you should apply on the field.

Do you know what your reputation is among players and coaches? Do you act to enhance your reputation? Florida's David Albany wrote an e-mail posting to a colleague and discussed how reputations form and how they can be destroyed or enhanced. Not all of his advice is by-the-book. Take from his writing those aspects that will work for you and incorporate those into your game management.

Rule changes, law changes, learning the secrets of veteran referees, bringing the answers to quiz questions to life — there's something here for everyone.

I've enjoyed the research that went into this book, but there are many others to thank. C. Cliff McCrath of the NCAA soccer rules committee and Alfred Kleinaitis, USSF manager of referee development and education, contributed to the technical accuracy of the text. I thank them, as well as the authors, for their contributions.

Good luck in your games ahead.

— *Carl P. Schwartz*, Referee *Associate Editor*

Chapter 1

1999-00 Federation Rule Changes

By Carl P. Schwartz

The National Federation of State High School Associations (NFHS) soccer rules committee made few rule changes this year. They gave states more control on deciding how to break ties at the end of 80 minutes. They also made one change to bring the game closer to the FIFA *Laws of the Game*.

Federation-registered referees should attend state association training and follow state interpretations or explanations.

Socks (4-1-1a).

"Effective 2000-01, both stockings shall be the same color, shall be the same single dominant color and not necessarily the color of the jerseys." That eliminates "bumble-bee" socks.

Although the rule change will not be in effect for the coming season, by including it this year, the change allows schools to budget for and obtain legal socks.

The change benefits referees. When you judge contested balls in a jumble of players, if you see an unfair action, you want to penalize the offending team. If all the socks are the same color (unthinkable in many European nations) or an assortment of colors, it makes your decision far more difficult.

Tie games (7-3-1).

"Regular-season games which are tied at the end of 80 minutes of play may be resolved by procedures adopted by state high school associations." NOTE: "No overtime procedures shall exceed 20 minutes of play during the regular season."

With a variety of options available, each state's governing body must decide what is most proper for their circumstances. Golden-goal, full length overtimes, shots from the penalty mark or letting the tie stand are all viable choices. Referees must know the proper procedure before the game. Many referees cover that subject with captains during the pregame coin toss to eliminate any uncertainty before the match starts.

Referees must know if the regular-season procedures differ from the tournament progression procedures. Also, you must know if the junior varsity games go to a tiebreaker. While most states and conferences do not want tie games broken at the sub-varsity level, eliminate the possibility of screaming coaches and unpleasant scenes by knowing what the conference wants ahead of time. It's best to have it available in writing.

> *Play 1:* A junior varsity match ends with the score tied, 2-2. The referees prepare for the varsity contest. The coach of team B screams at the referees from 45 yards away, "That's not right. My girls want to play overtime and decide this. I called the commissioner and she said we play overtime." The referees consult the written conference ruling distributed during the preseason and discover overtime is not played during junior varsity contests. The sheet explains the ruling by saying the varsity contest should start as close to the scheduled starting time as possible.

Ruling 1: The referees continue to prepare for the varsity contest. The referee of the junior varsity game reports the misconduct of the team B coach to the state association. The telephone call between the team B coach and the commissioner has no effect on the decision. If the commissioner wanted overtime to decide a tie match, the referee should have been notified directly or had the decision available in writing at the game site. (7-3-1, 12-8-1f)

Play 2: The varsity game ends with the score tied, 3-3. The coach of team B, a former professional player, wants to play a 30-minute mini-game, as he did in his playing days.

Ruling 2: Improper procedure. No overtime may exceed 20 minutes. Follow the guidelines in your printed state association handouts and explained during your preseason training sessions.

Goalkeepers given time limits (12-7-5).

In a change to the wording, the rule now reads: "A goalkeeper shall release the ball into play within five seconds after taking possession/control." Previously, the wording was the keeper "shall not indulge in tactics which ... are designed to waste time."

That change speeds up play and comes closer to FIFA law. FIFA allows five to six seconds. The NCAA allows five seconds. Having the ball out of the goalkeeper's hands and at the feet of the field players demands more fitness on your part. Prepare for it.

Do not begin counting the five seconds the instant the goalkeeper touches the ball after making a difficult or diving save. Especially if the keeper is in a crowd of players or an opponent looms over the keeper's prone body, allow the keeper a moment to assess the field and regain control over her body.

Also, do not visibly or verbally count the five-second period.

You may have witnessed referees in the National Professional Soccer League (NPSL, an indoor league) make an arm motion to indicate the passing time. Unless you are an NPSL referee working an NPSL match, make no motion or verbal count.

New field construction (1-1-1 NOTE).

"The committee approved a recommendation that states: 'When designing a new athletic facility, consideration should be given to broken-back type curve tracks to accommodate soccer fields. Broken-back tracks are oval in nature and can accommodate wider soccer fields.'"

Unless you serve on your local school board, you have little input to new construction. However, this note benefits referees in several important ways. Like the current Pontiac commercials suggesting that, "Wider is better," a wider soccer field allows more open play. If the players use that width properly, there are less contact situations for you to judge and less fouls to whistle. Players have time to decide their next course of action and do not get as easily frustrated. Overall, there is less dissent on a wider field because referees are less of a determining factor in wide-open play.

Chapter 2

1999 NCAA Rule Changes

By Carl P. Schwartz

The NCAA men's and women's soccer rules committee made only minor modifications to the game during their Feb. 2-5 meeting in Palm Springs, Calif. In the most dramatic change, all overtime periods become sudden victory. Previously, regular-season games ended with a golden goal but postseason games had two complete 15-minute periods before two 15-minute sudden victory periods.

Consult the official NCAA rulebook for late-breaking information and paragraph numbering changes. Attend National Intercollegiate Soccer Officials Association (NISOA) preseason meetings for in-depth coverage of the changes and inter-pretations presented by qualified instructors and clinicians.

Referee thanks C. Cliff McCrath, NCAA soccer committee secretary-rules editor, and the *NCAA News* for the information used to compile this chapter.

The committee discussed the differences in pregame administration between different institutions. The committee recommended the use of a pregame timing sheet for pregame administration. The NCAA will produce a sample timing sheet to assist those teams unfamiliar with its use. The committee anticipates stricter adherence to timely roster exchanges (3-2) and game start times. Referees working USSF professional division matches are familiar with the pregame timing sheets.

Logo restrictions (4-1).

The committee also added language to the rulebook concerning the new logo restrictions of team bench personnel participating in NCAA championships or media conferences. Bylaw 12.2.2, which applies to the logo restrictions of student-athletes' apparel, was expanded to cover coaches, athletic trainers, managers, band members, cheerleaders, dance team members and the institution's mascot at NCAA championships.

However, the committee voted to allow players to wear a commemorative patch on the team jerseys. Specific sizes and limitations are not available at this time.

Pressbox (6-3).

The pressbox facilities are a permissible substitute for a timekeeper's table on the field.

Many of the larger schools already use the pressbox to house the scorekeeper, timekeeper, electronic scoreboard operator and other staff. Referees should note their location prior to the game and use hand signals to communicate with those other officials.

Boxscore form (6-4).

The committee determined that computer-generated boxscore forms are permissible in the scoring of NCAA competition. The list of scorekeeper duties reflects what statistical information is necessary on the score sheet being used.

Overtime (7-1).

A revised overtime policy may prompt coaches to change strategies should games require extra periods of play. The committee approved that all overtime periods in both regular-season and postseason play be sudden death.

The change was in response to requests from the National Soccer Coaches Association of America (NSCAA), who asked that overtime policies be consistent between the regular season and postseason. The postseason overtime procedure retains four overtime periods before going to penalty kicks, but all four periods are sudden victory.

Play 1: Ninety minutes of regular soccer passed, with the score 2-2. The referee brings the team captains together for a coin flip and states there will be two 15-minute sudden-death periods to determine a winner.

Ruling 1: Correct. The referee should allow the captains to hydrate themselves and then conduct the flip. The interval between the end of regulation play and the start of overtime shall not exceed five minutes. (7-2)

Play 2: In overtime, during the 97th minute of play, the home team scores to take a 3-2 advantage. Six minutes later, the visitors get a goal to even the score at 3-3.

Ruling 2: Incorrect procedure. As soon as the home team scored, the game is over. (7-1a)

Play 3: After 120 minutes of soccer in a regular-season game, the score remains 2-2. The referee signs the boxscore form declaring the game a draw.

Ruling 3: Correct. The official scorer shall obtain the referee's signature on the boxscore form to verify cards issued, ejection reports and the official score. (6-4, 7-1 AR 1)

Goalkeeper may not catch throw-in (12-11).

A goalkeeper may not catch a throw-in directly from a teammate. That is now consistent with other rulemaking bodies.

> *Play 4:* Goalkeeper A1 catches the ball in both hands after it was: (a) thrown in by A6 or (b) headed to A1 by A7 after a throw-in by A8.
>
> *Ruling 4:* Illegal in (a). Award an indirect free kick to team B from the location where A1 handled the ball, unless A1 is standing inside the goal area. In that case, move the ball to the goal area line parallel to the goalline, six yards from the goalline. In (b), continue play. The intervention by A7 allows A1 to handle the ball, unless it is deliberately kicked to A1. (12-11, 12-11c, 13-2)

Cautions

The committee reviewed preliminary research on the possible implementation of a card-monitoring system but agreed that a card-monitoring system was not necessary at this time.

Both yellow and red cards were monitored by Dr. Joe Bean in the 1980's and reports broke the cards down into various categories: time issued, by state, by division, etc. The number of cards issued grew to the point where that became unmanageable. Now, only red cards are reported to Mr. Layton Shoemaker who compiles a report for NISOA, NSCAA and the rules committee.

The committee also dealt with issues relating to cautions and ejections. They reiterated that if a player receives a caution during a game, the only other card that player might receive in that game is a red card, regardless of the severity of the player's second offense.

The committee issued the clarification to address confusion regarding players who commit two "yellow-card offenses" during the same game. The committee emphasized that even though the offenses, had they occurred in separate games would have been classified as a yellow-card offenses, the second card issued to the same player in a single game is always a red card. For accumulation purposes, the most cards any one player may receive in a game is one yellow followed by one red.

Play 5: In the 25th minute, A4 is guilty of incidental profane language and the referee displays a yellow card. Shortly after restarting the second half, the coach of team A realizes the team only has 10 players on the field. The coach shouts at A4, sitting on the bench, to get onto the field as A4 was supposed to be a second-half starter. A4, without reporting to the referee or assistant referee sprints onto the field as ordered by the coach. The referee notices A4 sprinting onto the field, stops play and walks toward A4. Quickly realizing A4 already has a caution and not wanting to punish the team so severely for a non-contact infraction, the referee displays a yellow card to A4.

Ruling 5: Incorrect procedure. Show A4 the red card. Any player who persists in misconduct after receiving a caution must be ejected.

The fact that the second caution is a non-contact incident and is a technical violation of the playing rule is not a factor. A4's actions in the 46th minute deserve a caution. (5-4 AR 14, 12-14a, d, 12-15c)

Play 6: In the 18th minute, A8 receives a caution for unsporting conduct after a reckless contact foul against B5. A8 continues to play in an overly aggressive manner. No single foul is sufficient to caution A8 for persistent infringement but the referee senses that soon stiffer action will be needed to maintain game control. The referee informs playing captain A10 of those facts.

Ruling 6: Correct procedure. That is preventive officiating. Armed with the proper information, A10 can make the right decision. A10 may talk to A8 or the team A coach to settle the aggressive behavior. A12 may replace A8 so that A8 does not commit a second yellow card offense in that game. (5-5b, AR 10, 12-14e)

Cautionable offenses (12-14).

Players delaying the restart of play or players failing to respect the required distance when play is restarted with a corner or free kick are added to the list of cautionable offenses. That is now consistent with the international rulemaking body.

Play 7: The referee awards team B a direct free kick 25 yards from the team A goal. A4 runs 30 yards to kneel within four yards of the ball to untie and retie a shoelace. As the referee reaches for the yellow card, the player exclaims, "But referee, my shoe was about to fall off." The referee stops the clock, displays the yellow card to A4 and reminds A4 that further acts of misconduct shall result in ejection.

Ruling 7: Correct procedure. In previous years, that behavior was still cautioned as an incident of unsporting conduct. That change more specifically identifies the reason for caution. The offenses are unchanged.

Referees must realize that allowing players to prevent quick restarts or inject wasted time into a game penalizes the other team twice. In play 7, the referee awarded a direct free kick to team B because a team A player committed a foul. That free kick restores a fair balance because A9 committed an unfair act. Allowing A4 to further penalize team B by making them wait until the defense is set is a second injustice that needs remedy. The caution is a formal disciplinary action, visible to all, that such misconduct must cease. Allowing a team with a slim winning margin to waste time frustrates the losing team, which may react with reckless personal challenges against players wasting time. Do not allow players to delay the restart of play.

Ejections (12-17).

If a coach who coaches both a men's and women's team at the same institution receives an ejection, the coach sits out the next game for whichever team is being coached at the time of the ejection. The committee also emphasized that a coach serving a game suspension may not communicate or make contact with the team, assistant coaches or bench personnel from the start of the contest to its completion.

Penalty kick (14-4).

The committee revised the interpretation of when a ball is considered dead during a penalty kick after the expiration of time. The ball is live until the ball comes to a stop, regardless of any incidental contact with the goalkeeper.

Goalkeeper taking throw-in (15-2).

In an editorial change, the 1998 rule change stating that the player taking the throw-in may not use stickum or adhesive materials to enhance the grip on a throw-in applies to goalkeepers as well. In the rare case that a goalkeeper desires to take a throw-in, the goalkeeper must remove the specialized gloves that enhance the grip.

Throw-in against an opponent (15-2 AR 9).

The committee reaffirmed the approved ruling, denying the possibility of a player throwing a ball into an opponent's back and continuing play with the rebound. While the international laws ask the referee to judge the overall action (severity of the throw), the rules committee is concerned with the emotions of the collegiate player and hoped to prevent flare-ups of an unsporting nature in a tightly contested match.

Actions of the soccer committees

The Division I men's soccer committee asked NISOA to "increase control of bench decorum and conduct." Further, the coaches can nominate officials to work postseason tournaments through the conference official's supervisor and their conference coaches group. Lastly, during tournament play an athletics administrator must travel with the team and serve on the games committee. The games committee consists of one representative from each school, the NCAA site supervisor and the referee.

The Division I women's soccer committee noted that the cable television ratings for the 1998 soccer championships were the third highest of all fall championships. The committee will use NISOA regional coordinators to make preliminary-round assignments based on input from local assignors, the regional advisory committee and NISOA-run clinics.

Both the men's and women's Division II soccer committees agreed to work more closely with NISOA to select championship officials. The men's committee also voted to prefer grass fields measuring at least 70 yards by 115 yards for championship sites.

The Division III women's committee was asked to be more sensitive to the college affiliations of officials when assigning officials to championship play. NISOA presented a discussion on identifying the best officials to work championship play. The committee discussed the role of the fourth official.

Chapter 3

1999 FIFA Law Changes

By Carl P. Schwartz

The 113th annual meeting of the International Football Association Board (IFAB) was held in the Vale of Glamorgan, Wales, on Feb. 20, 1999. While a number of proposals for changes to the laws were put forward for discussion, only the actual amendments are listed below.

Referee thanks Alfred Kleinaitis, USSF manager of referee development and education, for reviewing the material before publication.

The amendments to the laws come into force on July 1, 1999, or later as directed by your state referee administrator (SRA). If you are traveling outside your state to participate in a tournament, after getting your SRA's approval to travel, make certain you know if the new rulings apply.

Notes on the Laws of the Game

Before the table of contents, there are several notes. One of them changes this year:

"Subject to the agreement of the national association concerned and provided the principles of these laws are maintained, the laws may be modified in their application for matches for players of under 16 years of age, for women players and for veteran players (over 35 years).

Any or all of the following modifications are permissible:

- size of the field of play
- size, weight and material of the ball
- width between the goalposts and height of the crossbar from the ground
- duration of the periods of play
- *substitutions"*

Reason: The new wording allows the right to use flying substitutions only for the above-mentioned categories (i.e., U-16, women and veterans) and then only with the agreement of the national associations.

The USSF Memorandum says the term "flying substitutions" as used above refers to what is usually called in the U.S. "free substitutions" — unlimited substitutions with the right to return.

Play 1: In a youth recreation league, the referee notices A9 depart the field and A13 enter the field while the ball is in play. The referee stops play and cautions A13. The coach yells out, "Ref, we have to increase playing time somehow, so our board of directors said that was OK."

Ruling 1: The referee correctly applied the law. The league is not authorized to allow substitutions during play. Think of flying substitutions as free substitutions, allowing a replaced player to reenter later in the same match.

Play 2: In a men's O-40 league, in a one-referee system, player A8 wishes to enter after 22 minutes of play. A8 does not have a player pass to hand to the referee because A8 was a starter who departed the game after 12 minutes.

> *Ruling 2:* Correct procedure. A8 may enter the field as soon as any other player on team A departs the field.

The referee (5).

There is an amendment to point three under "Powers and Duties: Ensures that *any ball used* meets the requirements of law 2."

Reason: Following the introduction of the multiple-ball system now in use at major matches, the wording should reflect the plural rather than the singular "ball."

The USSF Memorandum says that attention is drawn to *Advice to Referees on the Laws of the Game* 2.1 which notes that "when more than one game ball is provided for a match, the referee must inspect all balls ... to ensure they meet the requirements of law 2."

> *Play 3:* Before a professional division match, the fourth official asks to inspect six game balls provided by the home team.

> *Ruling 3:* While law 5 specifies that the referee must ensure that the ball meets the requirements of law 2, the pregame inspection of the balls is typically delegated to the fourth official for professional division matches.

> *Play 4:* Ten minutes before a game, the referee notices a large pond near the north end of the field, directly behind the goal. The referee asks the home team coach for three game balls to inspect. Only two meet the requirements of law 2, so the referee asks the visiting coach to provide a game ball for inspection.

> *Ruling 4:* Correct procedure. To avoid lengthy delays, such as chasing a ball that settles into water or a thicket, referees should inspect several match balls. If the home team cannot

provide an adequate number, the referee should approach the visiting team to garner sufficient balls to keep the game flowing.

Fouls and misconduct (12).

A new IFAB Decision 6 was added: *"Any simulating action anywhere on the field, which is intended to deceive the referee, must be sanctioned as unsporting conduct."*

Reason: More and more players are trying to deceive the referee in an effort to gain a decision in favor of their team. Curb that trend. Any player attempting to mislead the referee must be sanctioned.

The USSF Memorandum says section 12.29.1 of *Advice to Referees on the Laws of the Game* lists a number of "specific actions considered cautionable as unsporting behavior," including "fakes an injury or exaggerates the seriousness of an injury" and "fakes a foul (dives) or exaggerates the severity of a foul." In response to growing concern over such behavior, the International Board has identified simulation of fouls to deceive the referee as a *mandatory caution* requiring display of the yellow card.

"Determining whether a player is seriously injured has become much harder now (that) there is so much play-acting specifically designed to mislead the referee. The general rule that those who moan and writhe are not badly hurt is a sound one. But if in doubt, and particularly if you have limited experience, give players the benefit of such doubt. That applies especially in the case of goalkeepers, as the team can be so vitally affected if they are genuinely injured and you allow play to proceed."

That quote comes from Jack Taylor, the English referee for the 1974 World Cup final between Germany and Holland. The amazing thing is that quote is extracted from his 1978 book, *Soccer Refereeing: A Personal View.* It becomes clear that referees must start to take stronger action now to eradicate the disease infesting the game. A well-placed yellow card, much like the one shown by FIFA referee Richard Grady during the April 3, 1999, encounter between the D.C. United and N.Y./N.J. MetroStars, will soon have diving and faking players play the game properly.

Play 5: After 24 minutes, A6 earns a yellow card for persistent infringement. Twenty minutes later, A6 screams and tumbles to the ground in the opponent's penalty area with a defender more than three feet away. The referee stops play, displays a yellow card to A6 and immediately displays a red card to A6.

Ruling 5: Correct procedure. A6 received a mandatory caution for taking a dive with minimal or no contact. Since that was A6's second yellow card of the match, the referee followed correct mechanics in displaying the yellow card first, immediately followed by the red card. Once A6 departs the field area, the referee should allow team B to restart with an indirect free kick at the spot where A6 went down. (Note: In matches played under Federation rules, allow a substitute for A6. A6 must leave the field.)

Play 6: With the score 2-1 after 86 minutes of play, A5 falls due to minor contact from B9. A5 lies on the ground, holding one leg, and begins to roll from side to side. The referee tells someone on team A to take the free kick.

Ruling 6: Correct procedure. Referees are to prolong a stoppage in play when, in their opinion, a player is seriously injured. With team A ahead by a slim margin in the dying minutes of the game, A5 is attempting to draw a favorable call from the referee by simulating a foul or by making minor contact appear more serious.

Referees now face a tough choice. A5 simulating a foul subjects him to possible caution for illegal tactics. Doing so causes the game to be held up for some seconds as the trainer comes onto the field to diagnose the extent of the injury and the referee records the needed information for the mandatory caution. That plays into the hands of A5. Directing a team A player to get the ball into play places those tough choices back on A5. Does he continue to lie on the ground as his team attacks for the insurance goal or does he stop his antics, spring to his feet and become a useful offensive asset?

The fourth official

In a minor alteration to the sixth bullet: "He has the authority to check the equipment of substitutes before they enter the field of play. If their equipment does not comply with the *Laws of the Game, he* informs the referee."

An additional duty given to the fourth official is that, *"He has the authority to inform the referee of irresponsible behavior by any occupant of the technical area."*

Reason: At the request of the IFAB, the national associations should appoint a fourth official to top-division matches in competitions organized by national associations or their leagues.

The USSF Memorandum says the purpose is to increase the responsibility of the fourth official and to give that person the authority to bring matters directly to the attention of the referee rather than requiring that all such communications go through the assistant referee.

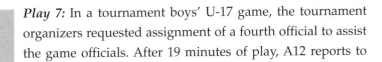

Play 7: In a tournament boys' U-17 game, the tournament organizers requested assignment of a fourth official to assist the game officials. After 19 minutes of play, A12 reports to

the fourth official for entry into the match. The fourth official takes A12 player's pass and substitution ticket and notices A12 is not wearing any shinguards. The ball goes out for a goalkick and the coach of team A yells to the referee for a substitution. The referee is about to beckon A12 onto the field but sees the fourth official holding a palm up (like a stop sign) and then bending to tap his shins twice. The referee does not allow the substitution and directs team B to take the goalkick.

Ruling 7: Deny A12's entry into the game until properly equipped. The fourth official might also inform both coaches to refrain from calling for substitutions and allow the fourth official to handle those matters.

Play 8: During a heated D-3 Pro match, someone on the team A bench throws a water bottle at the nearside assistant referee. Neither the assistant nor the referee saw who threw the bottle. At a stoppage for a throw-in seconds later, the referee asks the fourth official if she has knowledge of who threw the bottle. The fourth official said it was substitute A16.

Ruling 8: Correct procedure. The referee dismisses A16 for violent conduct and informs the coach of team A that team A is now limited to four named substitutes.

OTHER DECISIONS PASSED BY THE IFAB

Use of two referees
IFAB authorized FIFA to conduct an experiment in which two referees officiate on the field at the same time. The IFAB subcommittee will draw up the technical conditions for the experiment and FIFA will then choose the leagues and national associations that conduct the experiment.

National associations are reminded that no experiment of this kind may be made in any match without prior written permission from FIFA.

The USSF Memorandum says that although this experiment has been authorized, no procedures, techniques or mechanics have as yet been developed. All leagues, competitions and referees are reminded that the use of two referees is not permitted. Only the diagonal system of control (DSC) is authorized.

Play 9: During the girls' U-19 state cup championship final, the state president orders the referees to use the two-referee, two-linesman system. There have been several fouls behind play earlier in the tournament, one leading to a broken leg, and the president wants the security of an extra onfield referee.

Ruling 9: Incorrect procedure. The state president or the state referee administrator may not authorize the use of that system. The tournament must have the prior written permission of the USSF. Appoint a fourth official to handle many of the administrative matters and allow the assistant referees to focus more attention on player's conduct when the ball is at the other end of the field.

MLS makes a request

MLS commissioner Doug Logan stated in the press that he would formally request that USSF petition FIFA to be one of the leagues authorized to use the new two-referee, two-linesman system. At present, there is no further information on the request.

Fouls and misconduct

The IFAB wishes to draw your attention to the decision passed at its meeting on March 6, 1998: "A tackle from behind, which endangers the safety of an opponent, must be sanctioned as serious foul play."

IFAB notes that many tackles from behind have not been punished by the referee in the way dictated by that decision. Instructions will therefore be issued to monitor referees and any referee who does not apply that decision will be sanctioned.

The USSF Memorandum says that the International Board has emphasized the importance of carrying out its mandate to show the red card and send off the field any player who endangers the safety of an opponent by the use of a tackle from behind. Referees are reminded that, although that does *not* mean every tackle from behind must be punished by a send off, their discretion in this area is strictly limited to deciding if such action has endangered an opponent's safety. If it has, the player *must* be shown the red card. USSF joins the International Board in warning referees that their performance in that area will be monitored closely, with appropriate action taken for a failure to follow IFAB's mandate.

Recertification classes

USSF-registered referees are required to take five hours of academic training each year as well as a refresher test. Referees who have advanced beyond the entry-level are required to pass a fitness test comprised of four running elements. Certified instructors will cover these changes in detail during your training sessions.

Chapter 4

Flashback: 1998 Rule Changes

By Carl P. Schwartz

Here is a quick look back to the rule changes from the 1998-99 season. We offer these reminders as you prepare for the upcoming season. Paragraph reference numbers have been updated for 1999. Rulings shown here are still applicable.

FEDERATION

No markings on goalpost or crossbar (1-4-1).

No markings other than a single manufacturer's identification or logo may appear on the goalposts or crossbar. That is now consistent with the spirit of amateur competition and other rulesmaking bodies.

Play 1: During the pregame inspection, the referee notices the home team "Tigers" have painted a series of tiger stripes on all crossbars and goalposts. The home team refuses to make changes.

Ruling 1: The game shall not start. The referee shall make a report to the governing sports authority (athletic director or state association office) with jurisdiction over the game.

Medical bracelets taped to body (4-2-4).

Both medical medals (necklaces) and medical bracelets must be taped to the body. That makes the treatment of medical bracelets safer and consistent with the treatment of medical medals. Referees should concentrate on exposed metal and sharp edges, items that are the most dangerous to players.

> *Play 2:* During warmups, the referee observes player A7 with a metal medical bracelet on the right wrist and a leather "friendship bracelet" on the left wrist.
>
> *Ruling 2:* The medical bracelet must be covered with at least a single wrap of tape but may be worn during the game. The leather bracelet on the left wrist is considered jewelry and must come off if A7 wishes to enter the game.

Referee may stop play to remove player with dangerous equipment (4-3-1 Penalty).

The "Player Equipment" rule added a new provision: "... the referee may stop play immediately where there is an immediate dangerous situation." That change clarifies that referees can stop play immediately for imminent danger and eliminates confusion caused by last year's play ruling 4-3-1 Situation A.

Normally referees allow play to continue until the ball goes out of play to have a player correct equipment that does not meet rule 4. Asking a player to take off a watch, remove metal hair control devises or remove a visor may be done with the ball in play.

Kickoff in play when it moves forward (8-1-3).

For all kickoffs, the words "its circumference" have been replaced with "forward." The ball is now in play as soon as it moves forward, into the opponent's field of play. That is now consistent with other rulesmaking bodies.

Scoring directly from kickoff and goalkick (10-1-3a, c, 16-1-1).

In a move to increase scoring opportunities and encourage attacking play, teams may now score directly from kickoffs and goalkicks. That change is now consistent with other rulesmaking bodies.

Screening defined (12-5-2).

Although a player cannot legally "charge" an opponent from behind, a player not attempting to play the ball but remaining between the ball and an opponent may be legally challenged from behind provided the contact is not violent or dangerous and the ball is within playing distance. That change makes the definition consistent with the current definition of "charging" in 12-4-1.

That common-sense definition is now one of the clearest under any code. Referees have allowed screening (a legal practice) for years but have not had clear rulebook support for not making a call. The practical application has not changed: Screening is legal if within playing distance of the ball and contact from behind is legal until it becomes violent or dangerous.

Indirect free kick if keeper handles throw-in by teammate (12-7-4).

A goalkeeper shall not touch the ball with the hands or arms after receiving it directly from a throw-in by a teammate. The infraction will result in an indirect free kick, which will be added to the list of infractions in 13-2-2.

That change speeds up play and conforms to FIFA laws.

Play 3: Player A8 is awarded a throw-in and legally throws the ball to (a) A4 standing in the defensive penalty area, or (b) goalkeeper A1 who plays the ball with the feet, or (c) A1 who parries the ball with the fingertips, or (d) A1 who catches the ball and quickly throws it to A9, or (e) to A6 who heads the ball to A1 and A1 picks it up.

Ruling 3: In (a), (b) and (e), the action is legal and play continues. In (c) and (d), any touching with the hand or arm by A1 after the ball is thrown in by a teammate results in an indirect free kick at the spot of the touching unless the spot is inside the goal area. If the touch is inside the goal area, the ball is brought out to the goal area line parallel to the goalline, six yards from the goalline, for the indirect free kick.

Goalkeeper movement on penalty kicks (14-1-3).

On a penalty kick, lateral movement by the goalkeeper is allowed, but the goalkeeper is not permitted to come off the line by stepping or lunging forward until the ball is in play. That change is now consistent with other rulesmaking bodies.

Play 4: Team B is awarded a penalty kick. The referee properly sets everyone for the kick, blows the whistle for the restart and goalkeeper A1 (a) dives to the right as kicker B8 begins the approach, or (b) takes three paces forward before the ball is kicked and jumps to the right after the kick is taken. In both cases, A1 blocks the shot.

Ruling 4: In (a), the action is legal and play continues. In (b), the penalty kick is retaken because of the goalkeeper's violation.

Placement for corner kick (17-1-3).

Placing the ball on the line for corner kicks is legal. That change is now consistent with other rulesmaking bodies.

The ball must rest on the ground within the corner arc, including the width of the lines that enclose the arc. It is legal for the ball to extend beyond the corner arc area so long as it rests on the ground within the area.

Free kicks in play sooner (18-1-1r).

The definition of free kicks deleted the phrase "so that it travels its circumference." Also the committee added to the end of the last sentence: "The ball is considered to have moved when it is touched by the kicker." That change is now consistent with other rulesmaking bodies.

Signal for valid goal added. (Signal chart).

A commonly used signal for a goal has been added. The referee, after confirming the goal with all officiating partners, points to the center of the field to signify a valid goal. The timeout signal was not always sufficient for the timer and others to know a goal had been scored.

NCAA

Available shooters increased in tiebreaker kicks (7-1b).

The committee increased the number of players allowed to participate in the tiebreaker from those who have played in the game to any player listed on the official game roster.

Play 1: Player A18 twisted an ankle in the last regular-season game. In today's conference tournament game, A18 is listed on the roster but did not play due to the injury. After the full 90 minutes and two overtime periods, the score remains tied at 2-2. Team A's coach wants A18 to be the third shooter in the tiebreaker procedure.

Ruling 1: Legal. Although A18 has not played during any regular period or overtime period, A18 may take a kick from the penalty kick line during the tiebreaker procedure because A18 is listed on the roster.

Play 2: Substitute goalkeeper A22 did not participate during any regular period or overtime period, but when goalkeeper A1 is injured during the first kick by team B, team A's coach wants to substitute A22 for A1.

Ruling 2: Legal.

Card accumulation system same for coaches (12-18).

The committee reviewed the yellow and red card accumulation system and determined that coaches shall be subject to the same penalties and accumulations as players.

Play 3: Coach A enters the game with a season total of four yellow cards. In the 73rd minute, coach A is cautioned for dissent.

Ruling 3: Coach A may remain along the sideline for the remainder of the game, unless issued a second card. Coach A must sit out the next regularly scheduled game, including postseason games. This changes the ruling in AR 86.

Goalkeepers need distinguishing jerseys (4-2).

The rule requiring goalkeepers to wear colors that distinguish themselves from all other players and referees refers only to jerseys.

Play 4: Goalkeeper A1 has a gold shirt and black shorts while team A is playing in red jerseys. Team B is playing in green jerseys with black shorts.
Ruling 4: Legal. Although A1 has the same color shorts, the only requirement is for A1's jersey to be distinguishable.

Player repairing equipment (3-4h).

If a team substitutes for a player who is ordered off the field for an equipment change, the opposing team may replace an equal number of players at that time.

Play 5: In the ninth minute, the referee discovers A8's knee brace has exposed metal since the protective wrap fell off. At a stoppage for an unrelated direct free kick, the referee orders A8 off the field to repair the brace, and A12 comes on for A8. Team B's coach wants to substitute both B12 and B13 who have been waiting to get into the game.

Ruling 5: Not legal. Either B12 or B13 can enter the game at that point. The other team B player must wait for the next available substitution opportunity.

Handling the ball must be deliberate (12-3).

The committee changed "intentionally" to "deliberately" in 6-3 regarding handling the ball. This change brings NCAA rules in line with the other governing bodies.

Suspension being served in suspended game (12-18 AR 90).

An ejected player or coach, who is serving a game suspension in a game that is suspended before it has reached the 70th minute may, if eligible, participate in the next regularly scheduled game. But that coach or player must sit out the remainder of the suspended game when resumed.

Adhesives banned to aid throw-in (15-2 Note).

The use of adhesive material to enhance the grip during a throw-in is banned.

Play 6: A5 has a small cut on the left hand, covered with a Band-Aid. In the 14th minute, team A is awarded a throw-in and A5 executes the throw-in.

Ruling 6: Legal. Covering a wound with a protective wrap does not enhance the grip needed for a throw-in.

Play 7: On a damp, foggy day the referee notices A4 is wearing gloves that are discolored with a brownish stain. A4 is taking most of team A's throw-ins, no matter where they are on the field. When the ball goes out of play for a team A throw-in, the referee asks to see A4's gloves and recognizes they are covered with pine tar.

Ruling 7: Not legal. Award an indirect free kick to team B from the point of infraction. If A4's action is considered misconduct, caution A4 and display a yellow card. With some preventive refereeing, this illegal action will be caught early in the game and action taken to prevent misconduct.

FIFA

Referee decisions are final (5).

"Facts connected with play shall include whether a goal is scored or not and the result of the match."

USSF Advice to Referees: This arises from the statement in law 5 that "the decisions of the referee regarding facts connected with play are final." It is intended to confirm that the finality of referee decisions specifically includes goals scored and match results.

Indirect free kick if you stop play solely for misconduct (12).

"An indirect free kick is also awarded to the opposing team if a player, in the opinion of the referee:

• *commits any other offense, not previously mentioned in Law 12, for which play is stopped to caution or dismiss a player.*"

USSF Advice to Referees: The new entry returns to law 12 what had been clearly stated in editions prior to the general rewrite: When play is stopped *solely* to deal with misconduct (e.g., violent conduct, dissent, abusive language, and so forth), the proper restart is an indirect free kick regardless of whether the misconduct results in a caution or a dismissal. Referees are advised to remember that, if a foul is called in addition to the misconduct, the restart is determined by the foul.

Play 1: The ball is in play at midfield when B8, standing in the defensive penalty area, (a) swears loudly at the referee, or (b) punches teammate B9, or (c) pushes A10 to the ground.

Ruling 1: Indirect free kick in (a) and (b). The nature of both these offenses points toward sending off B8 for misconduct, but no foul was committed. The restart is an indirect free kick because the referee stopped play solely to deal with the misconduct. In (c), the restart is a penalty kick because the penal foul was committed by B8 inside team B's penalty area while the ball is in play.

Goalkeeper timewasting (12).

A new sentence was added to IFAB Decision 3: "The goalkeeper is considered to be guilty of timewasting if he holds the ball in his hands or arms for more than five to six seconds."

USSF Advice to Referees: This restriction on the goalkeeper was first stated as a "Mandatory Instruction" in 1997 and is now incorporated more directly into the law. According to USSF's Memorandum 1997, "Referees are reminded that their mechanic for measuring this time should not include any actions which would draw unnecessary attention (for example, audible counting or hand displays of elapsed seconds)."

Play 2: Goalkeeper A1 is holding the ball after a shot on goal. B10 is standing still, facing A1. After three seconds, A1 moves left to punt the ball upfield. B10 (a) stands still, or (b) moves right, into the path of A1, and A1 is not able to distribute the ball within six seconds.

Ruling 2: In (a), the action is legal and play continues. In (b), B10 commits an infraction. An indirect free kick is awarded to team A. Although technically this is the correct action, referees must understand this places team A at a disadvantage so quietly warning B10 not to repeat the infraction is appropriate.

New IFAB Decision 5 on tackles from behind (12).

"A tackle from behind which endangers the safety of an opponent must be sanctioned as serious foul play." This decision means that the player guilty of such an offense has to be sent off in accordance with law 12.

USSF Advice to Referees: This new language has received considerable public notice, much of it based on incorrect interpretations. The statement does not mandate a send off for every tackle from behind and it does not make all tackles from behind illegal regardless of how they are performed. Referees continue to have the full range of options available to them for dealing with actions that are careless, reckless or performed with excessive force. The IFAB has emphasized, however, that any tackle, *which endangers the safety of an opponent*, must be sanctioned with a send off for serious foul play.

Play 3: Attacker A10 sprinted past the defense after a long ball was played into open space. A10's first touch on the ball pushes it another 15 yards forward for an obvious goal-scoring opportunity, with only the goalkeeper to beat. Defender B4 is directly behind A10 and uses (a) a leg, or (b) an arm to trip A10.

Ruling 3: In (a) and (b), send off B4 for serious foul play and award team A a direct free kick. The slide tackle in (a) is an example of a tackle which endangers the safety of A10. The arm tackle in (b) is clearly a tripping foul performed with excessive force meant only to stop A10's run and goal-scoring chance.

That message is not necessarily new. FIFA submitted an item for discussion to the 1994 meeting of the IFAB that read, "The board was of the opinion that the provisions of the current *Laws of the Game* already ban tackles from behind which are unfair. Referees should be instructed to take stringent measures against this practice as it constitutes a serious hazard to players."

The penalty kick (14).

"A teammate of the player taking the kick enters into the penalty area or moves in front of or within 9.15 m (10 yards) of the penalty mark:

- the referee allows the kick to proceed

- if the ball enters the goal, the kick is retaken

- if the ball does not enter the goal, the kick is not retaken

- *if the ball rebounds from the goalkeeper, the crossbar or the goalpost and is touched by this player, the referee stops play and restarts the match with an indirect free kick to the defending team."*

USSF Advice to Referees: The new point emphasizes that it is proper to stop play and restart with an indirect free kick for failure to respect the required distance only if the ball goes to and is played by the infringing player. Referees should also note the guidance given in USSF's Memorandum 1997: the infringing player should not be cautioned even under these circumstances but only upon a repetition of the offense.

Kicks from the penalty mark procedure.

New text: "The goalkeeper who is the teammate of the kicker must remain on the field of play, outside the penalty area in which the kicks are being taken, *on the goalline where it meets the penalty area boundary line."*

USSF Advice to Referees: The new language defines where the opposing goalkeeper must be during kicks from the penalty mark. The IFAB intended that the goalkeeper should not be in a position to distract the goalkeeper defending on the kick and so changed the location from the top of the penalty area to where the penalty area line intersects with the goalline. The decision as to which side of the field may be used for the opposing goalkeeper should be based on the referee's position and viewing direction.

Other decisions

Method of injured players leaving the field of play.

The IFAB reiterated that injured players able to walk off the field of play should be encouraged to do so, especially if close to the boundary lines (it is therefore unnecessary to carry them off the field on a stretcher in these circumstances).

The IFAB also confirmed that when returning to the field, an injured player can enter the field from any point on the boundary lines if the ball is out of play. If the ball is in play, the player may only re-enter the field from a touchline. In each case, the player must await the referee's signal.

USSF Advice to Referees: The above statement is a straightforward description of what options for returning to the field are available to a player who left the field for an injury with the referee's permission but who was not substituted. Referees are advised to remember that such a player can return during play, but only with the referee's permission and only from the touchline. This does not apply to players instructed to leave the field for bleeding, for blood on the uniform or to correct equipment.

Chapter 5

Key Rule Differences

By Carl P. Schwartz

As you reach into your referee kit for the appropriate badge, you begin thinking of rule variations for that competition. You need to discuss certain aspects of match control during the pregame with your officiating team. Your ability to remember the correct ruling may be key to successful game management in a heated match. But there are so many differences. How will you keep them straight in your mind? This chapter will help you with the key rule differences.

Interscholastic and intercollegiate soccer have altered rules over the years to emphasize different aspects, such as sportsmanship, safety and differences in skill levels. FIFA changed the laws to increase scoring opportunities and to protect star players from the so-called professional foul.

The Federation and NCAA continue to make significant strides to more closely align their rules of competition with the FIFA *Laws of the Game*. That trend continues this year.

Administrative matters

Forfeits

FIFA: The referee is empowered to terminate the game

because of outside interference. The referee has no power to decide that either team is disqualified and thereby the loser of the match. The referee provides the appropriate authorities with a match report. (5)

FED: The team forfeits the match if a team has fewer than seven eligible players (3-1-2). The head referee may terminate the game if conditions warrant. (5-3-2b, 5-3-1 Situation D, 5-4-1 Situation A)

NCAA: The referee may forfeit the game to the opposing team under three conditions: a coach prolongs a discussion or refuses to leave the field at the request to do so; a team without prior notification or extenuating circumstances is not on the field, prepared to play within 15 minutes of the contracted starting time; a team refuses to return to the field within three minutes after being ordered to by the referee.

Officiating systems of control

FIFA: Use a single referee. Two assistant referees may assist and advise the referee. That is the diagonal system of control. The referee keeps time on the field. A fourth official may assist the officiating team. (Referee Administrative Handbook; Policy of Systems of Officiating Soccer Games).
On an experimental basis, the International Board is allowing certain leagues and tournaments to use the two-referee, two-line system. You may not use that system without the express written permission of USSF.

FED: The dual, diagonal or three-whistle system may be used. A timer keeps the time unless otherwise agreed. (5-1, 6-2-1)

NCAA: The diagonal system is preferred, but either the dual or the diagonal system may be used. The timer keeps the time unless there is no electronic scoreboard visible to spectators and bench areas. In this case, the referee will keep time on the field. The conference may designate an alternate official to assist. (5-1)

Overtime

FIFA: If no goals or an equal number of goals are scored, the game shall be termed a draw (10). Where tournament progression dictates a winner must be decided, play extra time if dictated by local rules, followed by kicks from the penalty mark, if needed. Only players on the field may participate in the kicks. (Kicks from the Penalty Mark)

FED: By state high school association adoption, regular-season games tied after 80 minutes may be settled in some form of tiebreaker. If the score remains tied, the game ends in a draw, unless the state association dictates a winner must be decided (7-3). Where tournament progression dictates a winner must be decided, play extra time, followed by kicks from the penalty mark, if needed. (A Sample Tournament Progression)

NCAA: Regular-season matches have two sudden death overtimes of 15 minutes each. If the game remains tied after two 15-minute overtime periods, it is a tie (7-1a). Teams still tied in postseason play will take kicks from the penalty mark to determine a winner. Allow all players on the official game roster to participate in a tiebreaker. Tournament or postseason progression is detailed in 7-1b.

Time of game

FIFA: Play two 45-minute halves. The referee has discretionary power to allow for time lost due to substitution or other cause. Halftime will not exceed 15 minutes. (7)

FED: Play two 40-minute halves. The clock is stopped for goals, penalty kicks, cautions and disqualifications, and when the officials order it stopped. Halftime is 10 minutes. (7-1, 7-2, 7- 4)

NCAA: Play two 45-minute halves. The clock is stopped for goals, penalty kicks, players being cautioned or ejected, television timeouts and when the referee signals for it to be stopped. Halftime may be as long as 15 minutes. (7-1, 7-2)

Field conditions

FIFA: The referee has the power to suspend play if the field becomes unplayable and decides whether to start the match based on field conditions. (5, Referee Administrative Handbook 3037)

FED: The host school shall decide whether the field and other conditions are suitable for starting the match. Once the match begins and until it ends, the referee shall judge whether the match may be safely continued. (1-7-1)

NCAA: Same as FIFA. (5-3, 5-5a AR 8, 10-9)

Fouls and misconduct cards

FIFA: Only card a player or named substitute. A player red carded before the match may be replaced. A player sent off during the match may not be replaced. (3)

FED: Players, coaches and bench personnel may be cautioned or disqualified. A yellow and red card disqualification ("soft red" i.e., the player may be replaced) is issued for taunting or a subsequent caution. A team can't substitute for a player who is disqualified during a period of play, but it may replace a player who is red carded during halftime. (12-8)

NCAA: Players, coaches and bench personnel may be

cautioned or ejected. A player ejected before the match may be replaced. (12-14 through 12-17)

Players and substitutions

Rosters

FIFA: Give player and substitute names to the referee before the match. Nominate between three and seven substitutes, based on competition rules. (3)

FED: Each coach submits a team roster to the officials at least five minutes before the match. (3-1-3)

NCAA: The names of players, coaches and bench personnel and a list of each player's total cautions and ejections must be given to the scorekeeper no later than 15 minutes before game time (3-2a). Players not listed on the game roster are not eligible to play. (3-2b)

Substitutes

FIFA: Allow between three and seven substitutes, subject to each league's rules. A replaced player may not play in the game again (3). A 1999 law change allows reentry in youth, veteran and women's games. See pages 21-22 for further details.

FED: No limits on the number of substitutes or reentries. (3-3-1)

NCAA: No limits on the number of substitutes, but players are allowed no reentry in the first half, one reentry in the second half, no reentry within the same overtime period. Allow the goalkeepers unlimited reentry as long as they reenter as goalkeepers. An injured player may be substituted for and reenter in any period if the injury was caused by an opposing player who was cautioned or ejected in connection with the injury. A player required to leave because of blood and the substitute are not charged with a substitution. (3-5)

When to allow substitutions

FIFA: Allow substitutions when play has been stopped after the player being replaced has left the field (3). (Editor's note: There are many differences at the local youth level. Be sure to check local variations for the competition you are working.)

FED: Either team may substitute between periods, on a goalkick, when a goal is scored, when an injured player is attended to on the field, when a player is cautioned or when a player is disqualified. Teams gaining possession of the ball may substitute on a throw-in or corner kick. For entry on a throw-in, goalkick or corner kick, the substitute must have reported to the scorer before the dead ball. Coaching instructions shall not be given to players of either team when coaches or medics attend to an injured player (3-3, 3-3-2, 3-3-2a, 3-4). If an injured player is attended to on the field, the player must leave the field and may be replaced. (3-3-2a)

NCAA: Either team may substitute on a goalkick, corner kick, when a goal is scored, when a player is ordered off for an equipment change or between periods. If a team substitutes for a player who is ordered off the field for an equipment change, the opposing team may replace an equal number of players at that time. In case of an injury or a cautioned player, only the injured or cautioned player may be replaced, with the opposing team allowed to replace an equal number of players.

Teams may substitute on their own throw-ins. The opposing team may do so only if the team in control of the restart substitutes. Substitutes must have reported to the scorer's table and be beckoned by the referee before entering the field. (3-4)

Suspension of play

FIFA: After a temporary suspension of play for any reason not mentioned in the laws, the restart is a dropped ball. (8)

FED: After a temporary suspension of play for any reason not mentioned in the rules, restart the game with an indirect free kick by the team clearly in possession. If there was no clear possession, restart play with a dropped ball between two opposing players. (9-3-1)

NCAA: Restart the game with an indirect free kick by the team clearly in possession. If there was no clear possession, restart play with a dropped ball. (9-3b)

Throw-ins

All codes agree on certain elements: the thrower may not score directly from a throw-in; the thrower must face the field of play; have part of both feet on the ground on or behind the touchline; deliver the ball from over and behind the head; the thrower may not play the ball twice in succession; the throw must be taken from the location where the ball crossed the touchline; and the ball is in play as soon as any part of the ball breaks the plane above any part of the touchline.

FIFA: FIFA only says that the thrower must use both hands. (15) *Advice to Referees on the Laws of the Game* 15.3 allows a player who lacks the normal use of one or both hands to perform a legal throw-in if the ball is delivered over the head. "There is no requirement in law 15 prohibiting spin or rotational movement. Referee must judge the correctness of the throw-in solely on the basis of law 15."

FED: In addition, the thrower must "use both hands with equal force ... in one continuous movement." (15-1-2)

NCAA: The thrower "shall use both hands equally." (15-2)

Chapter 6

Quiz and Mechanics

By Richard Arnold

In each of the following, you read a situation and several possible answers. Decide which answer or answers are correct for 1999 FIFA laws and Federation and NCAA rules. The correct answers follow each question along with the mechanics referees and assistant referees should follow.

Play 1: During play, A4 chest traps the ball, flicks it upward with a foot and then heads it toward keeper A1, who handles the ball.

   a. No violation has occurred.

   b. Restart with a dropped ball where Al handled the ball.

   c. Restart with a dropped ball where A4 flicked the ball toward A1.

   d. Restart with an indirect free kick for team B

   e. Restart with an indirect free kick for team B where A4 flicked the ball toward A1.

   f. Restart with a direct free kick for team B where Al handled the ball.

   g. Restart with a direct free kick for team B where A4 flicked the ball toward A1.

   h. Caution A4 for unsporting behavior.

   i. Caution Al for handling the ball.

Ruling 1 — FIFA - e, h (12 Cautionable offenses 1); **Fed - f** (12-7-3 Note, Play Ruling 12-7-3 Situation A); **NCAA - a** (12-11c-2).

Mechanics: Because the three codes (FIFA, Federation and NCAA) differ on the infraction, it makes it difficult for officials who do youth, high school, college and adult matches. Since referees are the authorities on the laws, can you imagine how confused the players, coaches and spectators are? Teenagers who play high school soccer and on weekends play youth soccer often give up on knowing the laws or they try to manipulate one code against the other to get what they want. That brings on a possibility of dissent.

To minimize the dissent, I try to verbalize. When A4 flicks the ball up with a foot and maneuvers to head the ball, I know A4 is not going to clear it or dribble it. That leaves only one possibility of playing the ball to the keeper. In college matches, I wait until it has been headed and then I warn the keeper about picking it up. In matches, I try to warn A4 before the ball is headed. Usually that disrupts the heading. Since A4 was not under pressure to begin with (A4 had the time to juggle the ball up to head it), A4 can now change plans and dribble or pass to someone else. The result: you prevented the problem.

Play 2: A8, while dribbling the ball, leaves the field to run around an opponent near the touchline.

   a. No violation has occurred.

   b. Restart with a dropped ball where A8 left the field.

   c. Restart with an indirect free kick for team B where A8 left the field.

   d. Restart with a direct free kick for team B where A8 left the field.

   e. Caution A8 for deliberately leaving the field without the referee's permission.

Ruling 2 — All - a (FIFA 12; Fed 12-8-1a; NCAA 3-6 AR 31).

Mechanics: There is no violation when A8 leaves the field while running around an opponent. According to *Advice to Referees on the Laws of the Game* 3.9, "If a player in possession of or contesting for the ball passes over the touchline or the goalline without the ball to beat an opponent, he is not considered to have left the field of play without the permission of the referee. This player does not need the referee's permission to return to the field."

Changing the scenario slightly, what if opponent B6 trips A8 while A8 is off the field? It would not be a foul because the incident occurred off the field of play. To whistle a foul, the action must be committed by a player while the ball is in play, against an opponent and on the field of play. However, it is misconduct and should be sanctioned. Under FIFA laws, the restart for play stopped solely to deal with misconduct committed off the field is a dropped ball where the ball was when play was stopped, unless the ball was inside either goal area. Federation 12-8-3 Situation A and NCAA 12-14 AR 57 call for an indirect free kick from the spot of the ball at the time of the stoppage.

Play 3: A8 takes a penalty kick during extended time. The ball travels across the goalline after bouncing off the crossbar, drops to the ground and rebounds into the goal. As a result:
  a. No goal is scored.
  b. A8 must retake the penalty kick.
  c. A goal is scored.
  d. Any team A player may retake the penalty kick.

Ruling 3 — All - c (FIFA 14; Fed 14-1-6, Play Ruling 14-1-6 Situation A; NCAA 14-4).

Mechanics: Since the penalty kick comes during extra time, save yourself the possibility of some of the problems of a penalty kick. While the *Advice to Referees on the Laws of the Game* 14.8 says, "The referee has no authority to make the players leave the field or the vicinity of the penalty area for the taking of a penalty kick in extended time," taunting, striking opponents and encroachment can be avoided if the trailing assistant referee is positioned near the penalty area. Since the penalty kick is during extra time, those players cannot play any rebounds. They can only cause problems. Remind the players that they cannot play any rebounds so there is no need to race in for a rebound. Then tell the trailing assistant, "Keep an eye on things here." That serves to warn the players, remind the assistant and prevent the problems.

Play 4: A7, while within playing distance of the ball and able to play the ball, shields the ball preventing an opponent from playing the ball. As a result:

    a. No violation has occurred.

    b. Team B is awarded an indirect free kick.

    c. Team B is awarded a direct free kick.

Ruling 4 — All - a (FIFA 12; Fed 12-5-2, 18-1-1kk; NCAA 12-8 AR 20).

Mechanics: The problem with shielding is that you have to decide how hard you will allow an opponent to charge. As a general principle, the older, more-skilled players are permitted a harder charge unless the field conditions (wet, muddy or snowy surface) make that unsafe.

    The tone of the match also has a bearing. The more players are willing to accept your decision on other hard challenges lets you allow a harder challenge here. It is also a matter of consistency — what have the players come to expect during that game? If they are challenging you for control of the match, you have to tighten up and not allow harder challenges. It is critical that you immediately deal with any charge directed at the middle of the back of the shielding opponent.

Play 5: A8 is ahead of the ball, closer to B's goalline than the second-to-last defender, and intercepts the ball from a pass between two team B players. The correct decision is:

    a. Offside position and the offside infraction is penalized.

    b. Offside position but there is no offside infraction.

    c. A8 is not in an offside position.

Ruling 5 — All - b (FIFA 11; Fed 11-1-3; NCAA 11-1, 11-3 AR 5).

Mechanics: Since an offside position is judged only from a teammate's touch on the ball and since it was the opponents who played the ball prior to A8's interception, A8 cannot be considered to be in an offside position. Without an offside position, there is no possibility of an offside infraction. However, there are likely to be some players, coaches and fans who expect and will appeal for an offside call. If a goal results from A8's heads-up play, team B players may dissent and cause bigger problems.

    Sell your decision. Since there is no offside position, don't keep it a secret. Tell everyone, "No offside, keep going" or, "Last played by an opponent, no offside." If the team B defenders quit now, they can only blame themselves for a bad play and an even worse decision. You prevented bigger problems by vocalizing your decision.

Play 6: A8 runs down the left touchline, nearer team B's goalline than both the ball and the second-to-last defender, when the ball is played forward by A5 down the right touchline.

    a. Offside position and the offside infraction is penalized.

    b. Offside position but there is no offside infraction.

    c. A8 is not in an offside position.

Ruling 6 — All - b (FIFA 11; Fed 11-1-3a Diagram 18; NCAA 11-3 AR 7).

Mechanics: The area of active play is a difficult thing to define because it "shifts, widens, narrows, lengthens or shortens, according to where the ball is going," says *Advice to Referees on the Laws of the Game* 11.3. The players' speed and skill, the playing surface conditions, field size and position of the players can affect that area where the ball can next be played.

For example, A7 is in an offside position seven yards outside the penalty area. A10 makes a through pass that goes within five yards of A7. There are times when A7 is in the area of active play and times when A7 is not.

Suppose that the players are younger and slower. The grass is short and dry. The through pass goes directly to keeper B1 who would rather punt the ball than put it down for an indirect free kick. A skilled assistant reads the development of the play and keeps the flag down while running toward the goalline, because the area of active play is more limited. Consider A7 outside the area of active play and thus A7 commits no infraction.

Suppose that the players are more skilled and faster. The grass is longer and will slow the rolling ball. A skilled assistant reads the play and judges that the rolling ball can be challenged by the offside A7. Before that challenge occurs, the flag is raised, the whistle blown and the challenge stopped because the area of active play is larger here.

Play 7: A6, nearer to team B's goalline than both the ball and the second-to-last defender, traps the ball from a throw-in by A4. The correct decision is:

a. Offside position and the offside infraction is penalized.
b. Offside position but there is no offside infraction.
c. A6 is not in an offside position.

Ruling 7 — All - b (FIFA 11; Fed 11-1-2 Diagram 16; NCAA 11-3 Diagram 18).

Mechanics: When signaling offside as an assistant referee, be careful to observe how the ball was played to the player in the offside position.

In a situation that I faced, the attacking team quickly picked up the ball for a fast throw-in. The assistant on the far side of the field didn't see the quick throw-in and raised the flag to indicate offside. The defending sweeper, B2, heard the flag and screamed for offside to stop the attack. Teammate B3 was obviously beaten and B2 would have to cover, leaving A11 open in front of the goal. Play continued because there was no offside and I waved down the assistant's flag. B2 ran toward A6, who then centered the ball for A11 to score. While team A was celebrating, several players from team B were in my face demanding the offside call. Others went over to my assistant to demand that the offside nullify the goal. The score was now 1-0 in the 87th minute. I was bumped by B2, who was sent off before order could be restored and the game finished.

Two weeks later the same thing happened on a quick throw-in and my assistant raised the flag. As before, I waved down the flag. That time, I called out, "No offside on a throw-in, keep playing" and the players did. The winning goal came in the 85th minute. This time, no one on the defending team contested the goal. There was no dissent at all. I avoided the problem by vocalizing and selling the call.

Play 8: A7 is nearer team B's goalline than both the ball and the second-to-last defender and steps off the field across the goalline as the ball is passed forward by a teammate.

    a. Offside position and the offside infraction is penalized.

    b. Offside position but there is no offside infraction.

    c. A7 is not in an offside position.

    d. A7 should be cautioned for deliberately leaving the field of play without the referee's permission.

Ruling 8 — All - b (FIFA 11; Fed 11-1-3, Play Ruling 11-1-2 Situations B and C; NCAA 11-3 AR 6).

Mechanics: A7 is demonstrating to everyone that A7 is not participating in the play. Similar acts of non-participation may include players turning their back, sitting down, raising their hands or standing like a statue. Stepping, running in front of or merely being in the way of an opponent trying to get to the ball is an act of involvement and must be penalized.

The potential problem is when A7 can re-enter. Must A7 have the referee's permission? No. What if the referee doesn't notice A7's departure or forgets about the player? How long should A7 remain off the field of play? Certainly as long as A7 is in an offside position by coming back onto the field. Should you caution A7 for misconduct upon entering without your permission in that case? I hope not.

When should the referee beckon A7 to return? Should A7 re-enter when goalkeeper B1 picks up the ball, remind A7 not to interfere with putting the ball into play. That avoids a caution for unsporting behavior and warns the keeper of the A7's presence. Should A7 get involved in the play, your caution is more acceptable because you took steps to avoid carding. Players will respect you for that extra effort. The rule of thumb — if permission is not needed to leave the field, then neither is it needed to return.

Play 9: A9 is 14 yards from team B's goal and receives the ball ricocheting from the crossbar after A11's volley from the 18-yardline (all team B players except the keeper are farther upfield than A9 when the shot on goal is taken).

   a. Offside position and the offside infraction is penalized.

   b. Offside position but there is no offside infraction.

   c. A9 is not in an off side position.

Ruling 9 — All - a (FIFA 11; Fed 11-1-3 Diagram 10; NCAA 11-1 Diagram 8).

Mechanics: If A9 does not make any affirmative action to avoid becoming involved in that play (turning a back to the play, kneeling, stepping across the touchline), the assistant's flag should go up. Wait for an indication of A9's involvement because A9 may have the self-discipline to stay out of the play and move away from the ball. What if A11 sees that A9 is in an offside position and can finish the original play? A11 calls off A9. A9 moves away and does not participate in play, while A11 runs onto the ball and shoots. An early offside flag adds to the defense's claim that A9 was offside and that the goal should be denied but that is an incorrect ruling because A9 did not participate in the play.

On the other hand, if A9 moves to play the ball or the rebound comes to A9, a strong flag helps speed up the whistle. It's unlikely the whistle will blow before the ball enters the net but the quicker the whistle, the less celebrating team A does. Then there is less problem denying the goal. Get team B to restart play quickly and keep an eye out to protect your assistant referee on that end. Also, keep moving to minimize dissent. If players have to chase you, they are less like to argue or complain. In addition, you are upfield to judge the next challenge better.

Play 10: A8 is nearer to team B's goalline than both the ball and the second-to-last defender at the time the ball was played forward by A10. A8 steps off the field to demonstrate uninvolvement with active play, then runs back onto the field 10 yards farther toward the goalline to control the ball, by which time both keeper B1 and defender B4 are now nearer to the goalline.

a. Offside position and the offside infraction is penalized.

b. Offside position but there is no offside infraction.

c. A8 is not in an offside position.

d. A8 should be cautioned for deliberately leaving the field of play without the referee's permission.

Ruling 10 — FIFA - a (11); **Fed - a, d** (11-1-3, Play Ruling 11-1-2 Situation C); **NCAA - a, d** (11-3 AR 6).

Mechanics: If players are cunning enough to use opponents and the touchline to put themselves back onside (which cannot be done), you are at a sophisticated level of play. The nature of that match warrants not only the offside infraction but possibly also a caution to A8. Advice to Referees 11.8 notes that a caution could be given for unsporting behavior for the sequence of actions if the referee believes it was done for tactical reasons or as a "feint."

Expect A8 to argue that the opponents caused A8 to be onside. You can minimize the dissent and gain added respect by being the first to speak. Tell A8, "You were in an offside position when the ball was last played by a teammate and sneaking back onto the field doesn't erase the offside." (Sneaking is the appropriate term because that is what offside was originally called. Players would sneak off the side of the field, hide in the crowd and race back on when the ball was played forward.)

Play 11: To start the second half:

a. The teams take ends of the field opposite to those they occupied at the start of the first half.

b. The teams remain on the same end of the field.

c. The kickoff is performed by the same team that kicked off to start the game, but in the opposite direction.

Ruling 11 — All - a (FIFA 8; Fed 3-2-2; NCAA 8-4).

Mechanics: Record on your game sheet which team gained the kickoff and what direction they kicked. Use a descriptive term such as north, south, toward the school or into the sun. Just before the start of the second half, look at your game sheet to see which team should kick off and in which direction.

Because of the 1997 FIFA law change to law 8, there is often confusion at the coin toss. What helps me is to ask captains winning the coin toss, "Which direction do you wish to attack?" They answer, "We want to defend this goal," and they point. I then tell the other captain, "You will kick off toward that goal," and I point. Then I record the team and direction on my game sheet.

Years ago, I was coaching a youth team. The captains returned from the coin toss perplexed. I asked which way we were going. One captain answered apologetically, "They're kicking that way." "Who won the toss?" I asked. "They did." Now I was puzzled and asked, "We wanted to go the other direction or kick. Why didn't we get either?" There was a pause and then, "They said they wanted to kick in that direction and the referee said OK."

Play 12: A7 takes a shot on team B's goal. The referee observes B4, standing in the goal area, reach out to deflect the ball from entering the goal. Although the ball is struck, the attempt is unsuccessful and the ball enters the goal. The referee should:

   a. Stop play upon seeing the deliberate handling of the ball, caution the defender and restart with a penalty kick.
   b. Signal that a goal has been scored, send off B4 and restart with a kickoff.
   c. Signal that a goal has been scored, caution B4 and restart with a kickoff.
   d. Stop play upon seeing the deliberate handling of the ball and restart with a direct free kick for team A.
   e. Signal that a goal has been scored and restart with a kickoff.

Ruling 12 — FIFA - c (12 Sending off offenses 4, Kleinaitis interp.); **Fed - b** (12-8-3a-1, Play Ruling 12-8-3 Situation G, Situation 18, 1992 National Federation News); **NCAA - b** (12-15 AR 65, 66).

Mechanics: If that shot occurs during the run of play or is a direct free kick, the shot on goal is a goal-scoring opportunity. There is a difference between FIFA law and Federation and NCAA rules. Under FIFA law, since A7 did not actually prevent the goal-scoring opportunity, the situation only calls for a caution. Both Federation and NCAA call for a disqualification or ejection because A7 attempted to prevent a goal-scoring opportunity. USSF guidance may be found in the "7+7" Memorandum and the *Advice to Referees on the Laws of the Game* 12.39.

Had that been an indirect free kick, there is no goal-scoring opportunity. If A7 does not handle the ball and the ball goes into the goal, it is a goalkick. That is one reason why you hold the indirect free kick signal until the second player touches the ball. If no one touches it, merely point to your raised arm calling out, "Indirect free kick, no second touch. Take a goalkick, defense." When A7 touched the ball into the goal, it is in effect an own goal. A7 became the second player to touch the indirect free kick, so award the goal. Let team A players chew out A7 and restart with a kickoff. No card is needed.

Play 13: The referee stops play for a foul by A3 near the penalty area line, then makes eye contact with the lead assistant referee to determine where the foul has occurred. The assistant referee should:

    a. Move directly to the goalline to indicate that a penalty kick should be called.

    b. Hold the flag straight up in the air with a brief back and forth motion to indicate that a foul occurred.

    c. Await the referee's decision, then confirm it with the

appropriate flag signal.

d. Stand at attention facing the field, holding the flag straight downward in front of the body to indicate that the foul was committed by the defense inside the penalty area.

Ruling 13 — All - d (FIFA *Guide to Procedures* 3L; Fed no written guidance; NCAA NISOA mechanics manual).

Mechanics: As an assistant, ask yourself, "Why is the referee looking to me after making the call. If the referee wanted my help with the foul, the eye contact should have come before the whistle." Right? The referee isn't asking for assistance with the foul, just the location. Is the foul in the penalty area or not? If the foul was initiated inside the penalty area, make the signal as described in answer d. If the foul was initiated outside the penalty area, stand at attention with no signal. That helps the referee know the foul occurred outside the area.

Remember, if the foul is inside the penalty area, the flag goes inside your leg. If the foul is outside the penalty area, the flag goes outside your leg.

Play 14: The only starts or restarts that requires the ball to go in a particular direction are a:

a. Dropped ball.
b. Kickoff.
c. Throw-in.
d. Penalty kick.
e. Direct free kick.
f. Goalkick.

Ruling 14 — All - b, d (FIFA 8, 14; Fed 8-1-3, 14-1-4; NCAA 8-2, 14-2).

Mechanics: Be vigilant at kickoffs and penalty kicks to make certain the ball moves forward. Be ready to stop play with a quick whistle and demand a restart if that does not occur. You may not award a free kick to the other team, as the ball was never properly put into play. The game *must* restart with the proper restart.

Some coaches are fond of using verbal deception on free kicks, corner kicks and even a penalty kick. One player placed the ball and "accidentally" tapped it just to move it. They would then call out to a teammate by name, "Fred, come and take it." Fred would slowly jog over. The defense would relax and Fred would immediately sprint toward goal, dribbling the ball. While physical deception is a part of soccer, such as a skilled dribbler faking out a defender, do not permit verbal deception.

Much of the rest of the world demands that a player calling for a ball must "put a name on it." Players must say something like, "Fred's ball." Merely saying, "I got it," to fake out an opponent from going for a header results in an indirect free kick. If that is done to deceive a keeper from going for the ball and allow a scoring opportunity, restart play with an indirect free kick after the shouting player is cautioned for unsporting behavior.

So if A5 taps the ball and calls out, "A10, take it," I call out, "The ball is in play." That removes the deception and preserves the equality by simply stating a fact. A5 has a problem. The opponents are usually closer to the ball than A10 and A5 cannot play the ball a second time until someone else plays it. Should A5 play the ball a second time, award an indirect free kick to team B from the place where the ball was played a second time. Team A usually stops the charade after the first occurrence.

Play 15: The referee applies advantage after A7 kicks B2. The benefit of the advantage disappears within the next two to three seconds. The referee:

a. Whistles to award a direct free kick if the foul was committed carelessly.

b. Can caution A7 if the foul was committed recklessly.

c. Can send off A7 if the foul was committed with excessive force.

d. Can do all of the above.

Ruling 15 — All - d (FIFA 12; Fed 12-8-1, 12-8-2; NCAA 5-3).

Mechanics: While the 1997 International Board decision allows a referee to whistle a foul after applying the advantage, referees have always been able to penalize misconduct by the next restart of play. A7 did not retain the benefit from the advantage call seconds before, so the referee correctly calls the foul.

Years ago, only intentional breaches of the law were whistled. Referees were penalizing "unintentional" fouls because they had an effect on the play and needed sanctioning. Often referees claimed that the so-called unintentional fouls were really better disguised fouls. To keep in line with the spirit of the game, the laws and rules changed to reflect that application. U.S. Soccer published a training module *Discriminating between Fouls and Misconduct*. I quote, "Forget intent — what counts is the result!" Careless acts are fouls. Reckless acts are cautionable misconduct. Contact using excessive force results in a red card. The codes changed to get in line with what was already being done by top referees. Several pages in the *Advice to Referees on the Laws of the Game* are devoted to that theme.

Play 16: Goalkeeper B1, within team B's penalty area, violently throws the ball, striking A3 who is standing outside the penalty area. The referee should:

a. Caution B1 and restart with a direct free kick to team A where A3 was standing.

b. Caution B1 and restart with a penalty kick to team A.

c. Send off B1 and restart with a direct free kick to team A where A3 was standing.

d. Send off B1 and restart with a penalty kick to team A.

Ruling 16 — All - d (FIFA 12 IFAB decision 1; Fed 12-1-3, 13-2-1c, Donnangelo interp.; NCAA 12-15a AR 60).

Mechanics: The question is, "Where is the point of the infraction?" The prior wording of FIFA law 12, International Football Association Board decision 1 was, "… if the offense took place in the penalty area." If B1 were to hold the ball and strike A3 with it directly, the goalkeeper would be penalized for handling the ball outside the penalty area before throwing it at an opponent (striking), so we are not talking about the same offense. Therefore, the question remains, "Where is the point of the infraction of striking. Is the point of the striking where the ball is thrown from or where the opponent is struck?"

Advice to Referees clears up any confusion for USSF referees in section 12.6: "Striking can include the use of any object (including the ball) as well as hands, arms, head or knees (if feet are used, the offense would be called kicking). In the special case of a player using an object (shoe, stone, etc.) to strike an opponent, the restart is located where the offense originated. Thus, a goalkeeper has committed a penal foul within his own penalty area and play is restarted with a penalty kick if he throws a ball with excessive force at an opponent standing outside the penalty area."

In the fall of 1989, an English referee faced an onfield decision. A defender inside the penalty area threw a shinguard at an opponent outside the penalty area. That referee awarded a penalty kick based on an earlier FIFA Memorandum identifying the point of the infraction of striking as being the place where the action was initiated. Unfortunately, in that same match, a defender had thrown a shinguard from outside the penalty area and struck an attacker inside the penalty area breaking for goal. The attacker stopped and the keeper gathered the ball. The referee decided to award a penalty kick because the punishment fit the crime. The protest by the defender's team was based on the earlier FIFA Memorandum. FIFA denied the protest. The next spring, a U.S. international panel referee had a similar onfield problem. In a Confederation-level match, a player took a legal throw-in, hurling the ball into an opponent's back. The referee judged that to be striking and awarded a direct free kick. But if the point of the infraction of striking was where the action was initiated (off the field), the restart should have been another throw-in for the same team.

In August 1990, Javier Arriaga of the FIFA referee committee was in Colorado Springs, Colo., at the State Instructors' course. I asked him about those cases. His response was, "FIFA has been inconsistent. We will correct the problem." Notice in the updated laws, the new wording of decision 1 for law 12. FIFA has gone back to the point of the infraction of striking is where the action originates in the case of a thrown object. That whole episode helped me better understand the spirit of the law: safety, equality and enjoyment.

Play 17: While holding the ball, goalkeeper A1 is injured and is unable to clear the ball. If the referee stops play for the injury while A1 still has control of the ball, the referee should:

    a. Restart with a dropped ball.
    b. Restart with a goalkick to team A.
    c. Restart with an indirect free kick to team A.
    d. Restart with an indirect free kick to team B.

Ruling 17 — FIFA - a (8); **Fed - c** (9-3-1); **NCAA - c** (9-3 AR 5).

Mechanics: Here is another difference between FIFA laws and Federation and NCAA rules. Early in my refereeing career, I thought FIFA should adopt the Federation concept of allowing an indirect free kick for the team in possession of the ball at injury stoppages. Then a senior referee explained to me that there was no need for such a change. According to the *Laws of the Game* and *Advice to Referees* 8.5, there is no requirement for two players to be present for a dropped ball. You may drop the ball for only one player, if necessary. If a goalkeeper is injured in possession of the ball and you feel it necessary to stop play, you may drop the ball for just the keeper to pick it up and punt it. That's what the keeper would have done anyway. That is more fair for the keeper than having to put the ball down and take an indirect free kick, which did not result from an infraction. It gives the opponents a chance to exhibit good sportsmanship. Notice that and praise them for their sporting behavior. Little things like that help with game control too. Federation rules do require two opposing players.

Quickly and quietly, administer that dropped ball when the keeper is ready to start. As you stand next to the keeper, ask, "Are you ready?" The usual retort is, "Yes." I answer, "When I drop the ball, pick it up and it's in play." Sometimes a keeper asks, "Can I punt it?" "If you want to," is my reply. I drop it and jog upfield by the nearest opponent and say, "Thanks for letting me drop the ball for the keeper to pick up. That was good sportsmanship on your part." Often they didn't realize what was going on but they still react positively to the praise. The referee has no official authority to prevent an opponent from attempting to take part in the drop, nor can the opponent be ordered away.

Play 18: Team A is awarded a direct free kick 20 yards from their own goalline. A3 plays the ball back, toward goalkeeper A1, who does not make contact with the ball. The ball enters the goal. The referee should:

    a. Award a goal to team B.

    b. Allow team A to retake the kick.

    c. Award a goalkick to team A.

    d. Award a corner kick to team B.

Ruling 18 — All - d (FIFA 13, 17; Fed 13-1-1, 17-1-1; NCAA 13-1a).

Mechanics: Since a team cannot score against themselves on a free kick, A3 has simply kicked a live ball out of play. Restart with a corner kick for team B. Team A loves that restart rather than the goal, so they won't say too much. Team B would rather have a goal (incorrect decision), so you need to sell the call to team B.

As the ball rolls toward goal, anticipate the possible problem. Race toward the goal too. As the ball crosses the goalline, give a strong blast of your whistle and signal sharply toward the corner. Then verbalize, "Corner kick since you can't score on yourself directly from a free kick." That minimizes dissent and improves respect because you hustled, were on top of play, made a decisive call and gave a brief verbal explanation. Now set up for a corner kick and encourage the players to do the same.

Play 19: A7's shot rebounds off goalkeeper B1 to A3, who was in an offside position at the moment of the shot. A3 controls the ball and plays it into team B's goal. The proper restart is:
   a. Kickoff for team B
   b. Goalkick f or team
   c. Direct free kick for team B.
   d. Indirect free kick for team B.

Ruling 19 — All - d (FIFA 11; Fed 11-1 Diagram 11; NCAA 11 Diagrams 6, 7).

Mechanics: I'll not reiterate the need for hesitation to judge involvement by A3 (see the response to question 9). You can gain much respect by praising the assistant referee at that point. Whatever the decision is in that case, letting assistants know that they made a great call is important. It reduces dissent from the players. It encourages the assistant to continue hustling and working hard to help your game. It also goes a long way to keeping officials from quitting. If they popped the flag smartly, give them a big thumbs-up and a loud, "Thank you." If they were a little slow or hesitant, blow the offside, race to the spot of the restart, look at the assistant and shout out, "Nice call," as you raise your hand for the indirect free kick.

Usually the assistant is the newer official in the crew and respects the center referee. Praise from someone you respect is highly valued. It opens the door to the best mentoring programs.

After the match, compliment both assistants on what they did well. Ask if they would like a suggestion to improve. If they say yes, give them one or two ideas to work on. Then ask if there is something they noticed that you could have done better. Listen and avoid justifying your actions. Consider their input and thank them. Those informal assessments go a long way toward helping newer officials develop skill and confidence. They stick with officiating longer and you gain respect in their eyes. Later, you will hear, "You taught the other official that trick and I learned it from them. Thanks."

Play 20: A9, playing with an existing injury to one arm, prepares to take a throw-in using only the healthy arm. The referee should:

    a. Allow A9 to take the throw-in using only one arm.

    b. Allow A9 to take an indirect free kick in place of the throw-in.

    c. Inform A9 that two hands are required when taking a throw-in.

    d. Require another team A player take the throw-in.

    e. Allow A9 to take the throw-in using only one arm and award a throw-in to team B upon completion of A9's throw-in.

Ruling 20 — All - c, d (FIFA 15; Fed 15-1-2-2; NCAA 15-2).

Mechanics: Between the printing of *Officials' Quiz: Soccer 1998-99* and this book, the correct answer under FIFA laws has changed. Authoritative confirmation of that is in *Advice to Referees on the Laws of the Game* 15.3: "A player who lacks the normal use of one or both hands may nevertheless perform a legal throw-in provided the ball is delivered over the head and provided all other requirements of law 15 are observed." Under FIFA laws, the correct answer is now **a**.

Referees can inform players of the laws and rules. Referees cannot determine where players play on the field or coach players, such as determining who should take a free kick, penalty kick or throw-in. I've seen referees lose the respect of both teams and coaches when they began coaching players on how to take a throw-in.

One official whistled an improper throw-in against the visiting youth team and then instructed the player that, "You'll be all right if you drag your back foot." The angry player shouted, "You're not my coach." The home team players questioned, "Why are you helping them? Whose team are you on?" As I ran the line, I watched both sets of parents get irate and mistrust that referee. Before the second half started, both touchlines had to be emptied. The home team demanded that the referee never officiate their games. The visiting team wrote a letter to the league complaining about the official. No one enjoyed the game that afternoon.

The best course of action — warn players about the laws. If a player then chooses to break the laws, the proper penalty needs to be enforced.

Chapter 7

One Referee's Reputation

By David Albany

(Editor's note: The following question was posed to David Albany, USSF State Referee from Florida, in a public forum and here is his multi-segment response. The two writers had exchanged previous Internet postings discussing referee professionalism.)

David,

You made the statement that I was endangering my "reputation" as a referee. I find the comment interesting because it challenged me to examine my reputation as a referee and what I want it to be. As referees, we serve different clientele — players, coaches and assignors. Should our reputation within each group be the same? My conclusion is that the most important aspect of one's reputation is that of fairness. If others perceive you as being fair, many other sins can be forgiven.

How do I want my reputation to develop? I want it to expand to where those same coaches, players and assignors begin to feel comfort with me as the center referee in higher-level matches. I earn that respect by improving my skills, speed and conditioning.

My response:

You wrote: "Should our reputations within each group be the same?"

That is a tough one. Some assignors feel that if you do not accept all the matches they assign you, they may not have you on their preferred list.

Whenever referees accept multiple assignments beyond their physical and mental engine, they face the virtually inevitable outcome: inadequate performance. I'm not talking about working five games at the U-10 level ... it's the competitive matches referees do without sufficient rest. You must understand that if you officiate more than two matches a day without a break, the third or fourth set of teams is not aware that you came to their match with an exhausted supply of energy. If you ruin their game due to your physical and mental fatigue, they will not give you an excuse for such: You will be the "worst referee they ever had." It may take you several future great matches to convince those teams that you are actually a good referee. However, because you were too tired during their games, you made mistakes and your reputation suffered.

You also wrote: "It challenged me to examine my reputation as a referee and what I want it to be."

The collegiate organization (National Intercollegiate Soccer Officials Association [NISOA]) and the professional organizations (Major League Soccer, A-League, United Soccer Leagues and National Professional Soccer League) are protective of their referees' reputations. They prohibit referees from doing other matches on the days they are assigned college or professional matches.

As I mentioned above, coaches and players do not easily forget referees who ruined their game. They may not always remember the good or great referee, unless you do their league repeatedly. Infrequently, you blunder. Look at (Italian FIFA referee) Pierluigi

Collina when he screwed up the match between Lazio and Roma during 1997's Serie A championships; Lazio coach Sven G. Ericksson said, "Collina ... *l'ultimo arbitro!*" He said Collina is the best referee ... and gave him a break for the mistakes he committed. Collina sent off an innocent Lazio defender, gave a yellow card for stopping an obvious goal-scoring opportunity ... it wasn't his day at all. Of course, Collina humbly admitted his blunders in a television interview.

When forced to take multiple matches, I tend to tell the last teams: "Hey guys, I'm dead tired, half my brain is dead. Please don't give me any grief and I won't give you any grief. We don't have fresh referees available for this game, so please leave my butt alone ... fair enough?" They usually give me the break I need. I usually call the game tighter than normal. I have to protect my reputation, right?

The assignor won't protect me if I mess up the third or fourth match ... he too tends to "conveniently" recall those bad games.

You worked so hard for so many games to make a name. When you mess up a game, others believe that it's not your fault if they can see you are overly tired from working a high number of games in a single day. Not long ago, two National Referee candidates asked the assignor to work me as their assistant. The first game was tough and fast ... I worked very hard tracking players. During the second game, I screwed up two offside calls plus a couple of other calls. Luckily, the innocent team won anyway. Some of the players said, "What's with Dave?" My reply was along the lines of, "Excuse me, I had no energy left for you guys." Luckily, that worked with those players. They knew me by name; I refereed them many times, both with and without assistants without any problems, so they gave me the break I needed. But the assignor put me in that position by scheduling two very competitive matches back-to-back.

Our contemporaries hear those stories through the grapevine.

"Hey, did you hear about Dave? He screwed up big time, gave 12 yellow cards and three red ones. He terminated a match after he assaulted three players. Then he assaulted a coach, and he … etc." Those statements tend to circulate rapidly. Nobody cares about the good games you have, of course.

The question is: "Why do you have to go that way?" You can minimize your bad games by being diplomatic with assignors. Ask them not to run you beyond your limits by working several competitive games a day. Again, fight the temptation to do multiple matches without rest.

You asked: "How do I want my reputation to develop?"

How do people selling a service want their reputation to develop? You must know your client. You must know as much as you can about your client, including the players, coaches and fans. When I work college games, sometimes the visiting team is from out of state. I know nothing about them. I go to www.<insert school name>.edu/soccer and read about their coach, their top players, recent injuries and anything helpful to my match control. Sometimes, I call a NISOA referee from that school's area to give me any helpful hints.

In a game when I was assigned as the assistant, I told my referee, "Watch number 14 and deal with him at the earliest opportunity. After that, you will have him in your pocket." Because I knew ahead of time what might happen, number 14 was correctly dealt with early. He behaved nicely for the rest of the game. In an earlier match, that same player pulled a few tricks on me until I booked him in the second half. He successfully manipulated me for over 60 minutes because I didn't have the proper information and he didn't know about my reputation.

Here are a few other affirmations that I've developed over the years. Those helped my reputation with players and coaches:
• Be kind to the underdog without affecting the outcome.

Kindness to the underdog does not mean cheating or not performing your job. It means you award more of those so-called 50/50 decisions in their favor; perhaps you cut them a minor break in non-crucial calls, etc. You never affect the overall flow of the match or the outcome. That approach is crucial for preventing fights in lopsided matches due to the natural frustration by the losing team. Awarding a couple of trivial free kicks in the middle stage of the game helps win the trust of the obvious underdog. Former Mexican FIFA referee Codesal awarded Cameroon a couple of trivial fouls against England in World Cup '90 in Italy; the kicks did not result in any tangible score, but Cameroon developed a trust for Codesal's style. Cameroon lost 2-1. In the English Premier League during the fall of 1998, a referee disregarded a corner kick for the team winning, 5-0, in the late stages of the second half. The losing team's keeper had just made an excellent save by deflecting the ball across the goalline. The attackers smiled and applauded the referee's decision for taking it easy on the opposing keeper, who was humiliated with five goals.

• If one team shows better compliance with the laws and plays with a sense of the spirit of the laws, take note of it. If one team exhibits a sporting approach, make more of the 50/50 calls favoring their direction. Deal with the misbehaving team players by using the letter of the law.

• After booking a very angry player, give a trivial call in that player's favor to regain some calmness.

• Use the stick and carrot approach. The wide scope of the stick and carrot approach is useful in all walks of life of humanity; the modern game of soccer shows referees various misbehaviors not covered in the *Laws of the Game.* Referees must be more than just law-enforcers. You must show inventiveness in dealing with gray areas of the penal code.

• Become aware of players booked in earlier matches, especially star players. Under some codes (college, professional leagues) players may be suspended for their accumulated offenses if you book them.

• Use your common-sense fairness when the *Laws of the Game* offer none. In an English Premiership match, referee David Elleray hinted to the coach that one player may need to be substituted to avoid the high potential for a second booking. The coach announced to the media his deep appreciation for such a cooperative attitude and Elleray's common sense.

• Keep communicating with players and coaches but do not argue. Your whistle and body language should be clearly understood by those on the field as well as those around it. Think about your body language as if you were on television.

• Do not explain your calls — use strong body language to deter such inquiries.

• Do not accept assignments if you're not fit, unless you don't care about your reputation and are in need of the game fee. Few referees can handle multiple assignments, yet remain physically and mentally fit.

• Acknowledge your errors to players. Fake arrogance gets you deeper in trouble.

• You need sufficient time to prepare mentally for your match. If you arrive late or you come to the match with a personal problem bothering you, your chances of a good game decrease. You're playing Russian roulette with your reputation. Life isn't fair —

the players remember and recall bad games more readily than good games.

• If a coach or team's influential administrator perpetually displays unreasonable behavior, you have the opportunity to blacklist that team. Bear one thought in mind: They are the ones who are desperate for your services.

When watching MLS games on television, pay special attention to Tampa Bay Mutiny forward Valderrama; he's a temperamental star player and does not like to be vigorously challenged. MLS referees need to be very careful in awarding advantage to Valderrama unless a goal is imminent. They need to let Valderrama see and know they are dealing with those who physically attempt to intimidate his superb passing skill. He once was sent off for retaliation after being fouled because the referee failed to punish the contact. Do not be too quick about giving advantage when a temperamental star is fouled.

Never compromise on a needed yellow or red card. It happened to me, and will continue to happen, although hopefully less frequently. In a high school match, I dealt with the earliest misconduct by lecturing the players. I was not aware that the victimized players did not accept my verbally admonishing the opponents. The match ended with 14 yellow cards, plus five opponents and the entire coaching staff of one team disqualified. Certain misconduct needs to be carded, especially early in the match, when referees tend to use verbal warnings.

Set reasonable goals and work hard to achieve them. Once you reach your goals, you will truly enjoy reaping the sweet fruits of your success. I set USSF State 1 Referee as my target grade. I reached it, later than I had hoped as it took me four years, but I'm now comfortable and enjoying it. Given my experience and personality, things flow at my own terms.

Find reputable referees, admired by players and coaches, and recognize their achievement and ask them for guidance and advice. Work with them. Ask if they will serve as your assistant referee on some games so you can experience how to work with veteran partners. Travel with them as they have tough matches and talk about soccer officiating on the way there. Talk about the game on the way back. Ask them to watch you, but then you have an obligation to listen to them and experiment with what they suggest. Ethics and their reputations bind certified assessors, so they are limited to what they can give you beyond the 15-minute debriefing. A friend, however, gives you a lot more ... if you can withstand a good but friendly ass-chewing approach.

If you reach State Referee and plan to go higher, it's time you slow down serving the youth game. You have sufficiently served the youth. It is now time to think about and study the top amateur and professional games. However, if your goal is to achieve State Referee and stop there, you must keep serving the youth game and be one of the many weekend warriors. Balance your time and energy among youth, amateur, high school and college games. Find opportunities to work youth and adult games, even at the expense of the higher paying college matches: Do not forget that youth and amateur games are the ones that gave you the experience to become a college referee. Do not dump them. I have no respect for referees who turn back youth and adult games in favor of college.

Don't ask for higher level games — prove your skill at the pitch. Let others speak of you and they will invite you to the big game. Do not go begging for big games. As an entry-level referee, do your best. You will be noticed and invited to upgrade. As a grade 7 referee, continue to do your best and in no time, assignors and assessors will ask you to upgrade.

(David Albany is a USSF referee who lives in Daytona Beach, Fla.)

Chapter 8

Case Studies From Two Decades of Soccer

By Richard Arnold

You've got stories to tell from your refereeing career. Even if you've only been officiating for a single season, events have come together to create a stressful situation. While traveling across the country over the past 20 years, certain memorable experiences have teaching points. Some are perfect examples of what not to do. They are presented in the form of case studies. Hindsight allows me to propose the solutions.

The Case of the Assertive Assessor

It is a hot day and the match involves arch-rivals. The referee finished the players' equipment check for team A (wearing black) and heads for team B (wearing white) to do the same. An elderly man with a clipboard shakes hands with the team B coach and then walks up to the coach of team A. The man tells the coach of team A that the goalkeeper must change the red penny covering the jersey. The coach of team A asks, "Who are you?" The aged man replies, "I am the assessor and the goalkeeper cannot wear the red penny." The coach responds, "You don't have any authority to make that decision," and turns to walk away. The assessor raises his voice, "I'll get the referee over here and make the keeper change." With rising irritation, the coach answers, "The referee has checked in the team and the penny was not a problem."

The assessor yells for the referee to come over and then demands the coach step away so they can converse. The coach tells the assessor, "If you're going to talk about my players, I'm going to be present." The assessor threatens, "If you don't leave now, I'll throw you out of the game." The coach stands silent, daring the assessor to do anything. The referee arrives at the confrontation. The assessor tells the referee to send the coach off because of interference with the referee team and the performance of their duties. Also, the assessor mentions that the goalkeeper is wearing an illegal uniform because it is not a goalkeeper's shirt.

If you were the referee being assessed for upgrade on that match, what would you do?

The Case of the Athletic Director

The high school league championship game is about to begin. The home team is heavily favored. The visiting team pulled two upsets to get to the title game. It's been a rainy day and the forecast calls for thunderstorms. The Cinderella team (team B) kicks off and attacks up the right wing. The ball is centered and home defender A3 slips on the wet grass. Attacker B10 heads the ball into the goal 30 seconds into the match. The home team is stunned and plays that way. Team B continues to dominate.

Five minutes into the match, the home team athletic director goes to the fourth official and says that the radio station announced a severe thunderstorm warning has been issued for the area. The athletic director wants the fourth official to stop the match for the players' safety.

What is the athletic director really trying to do? What should the fourth official do about the weather and the athletic director? What should have been discussed in that pregame?

The Case of the Guilty Victim

Team A's star attacker, A10, has already scored two goals and is giving team B defense great difficulty. At halftime, team B switches A10's marker to B3. Early in the second half, A10 is dribbling just outside the corner of the penalty area near the referee's diagonal. The referee has good position on the outside touchline side of the challenge. As the ball moves into the penalty area, A10 and B3 bump into each other. A10 starts around B3 but suddenly stops and pushes B3 to the ground. A10 yells at B3, "Let go of me." The referee whistles to stop play, awards a direct free kick in favor of team B and cautions A10. A10 complains that B3 was holding the jersey so A10 couldn't get to the ball.

What change should the referee make the next time A10 tries to dribble around B3?

The Case of Insufficient Information

Team A is attacking and B6 kicks the ball barely over the far touchline, on the side of the field opposite the assistant referee. A7 quickly picks up the ball and throws it toward A9, who is tightly marked by B2. A10 is just beyond them on the touchline, in an offside position. The ball bounces by the feet of A9 and B2, then continues to A10. Because the assistant referee is 75 yards across the field, she cannot tell who, if anyone, touched the ball. The referee is not in position to determine if A10 is in an offside position, but knows who touched the ball to A10. Neither official has enough information to make an offside determination as A10 races toward the ball.

As the assistant referee, you know that if A9 touched the ball, A10 is offside. If B2 or no one touched the ball, there is no offside. What should you do?

The Case of the Friendly Foe

Keeper B1 scoops up a through pass near the edge of the penalty area. Cross-town rival attacker A9 pulls up and stops right in front of B1, face-to-face. It is the third minute of the game and there have been no incidents so far. The two players exchange words and the referee begins running toward them. The two players smile and A9 pats B1 on the cheek. A9 turns to run away and B1 tugs A9's shorts, pulling them down about four inches. The two players laugh loudly.

What is going on between the two "rivals?" What should have been discussed in the pregame? Was there a foul or misconduct in that instance? How do you restart play if you stopped play with a whistle?

The Case of the Friendly Coach

As the officiating crew inspects the field prior to the game, the coach of team A approaches them. The coach introduces herself and carries on a friendly conversation. After several minutes, the coach of team B approaches. Just as the coach of team B arrives, the coach of team A leaves and reminds the officials that kickoff time is just minutes away and they need to start promptly.

What has coach A tried to do? Has a problem been created? Can you predict the coach of team B's reaction to the first controversial decision the officials make?

The Case of Touchline Friction

During a youth match, parents from team A are not only along their own touchline but positioned around the field on team B's touchline as well. They are cheering their children and calling instructions to players on the field.

How do team B's parents feel about having opponents cheer in their midst? Are team B's players confused because coaching from their touchline is not for them? What may happen if that continues? Does the referee have the right to control spectator behavior?

Answers

The following responses are not the final authority, merely recommendations. It is suggested that these case studies be discussed in referee meetings, in referee tents at tournaments, over dinner after games or in the car on the way to games.

The Case of the Assertive Assessor

Why does an assessor even talk to the coaches before a game? Why does the assessor treat one coach in a friendly manner and the other coach in a hostile way? The assessor has no authority concerning player equipment or to send off a coach.

The assessor has put the referee in a difficult situation before the match begins. The referee must have a challenging match because it is being assessed for upgrade. If the referee enforces the laws, the assessor is embarrassed and may respond with a failing assessment. If the referee sides with the assessor, there will be animosity and a protestable error in law application.

The referee must have the courage to do the right thing by the letter and spirit of the game and ask the assessor to refrain from interfering with the match participants (law 5: spectator interference). The referee must include the incident in the match report to the competition authority and send a copy to the assessor's superior (state or regional director of assessment).

The Case of the Athletic Director

The athletic director is applying some "gamesmanship" and really wants the match halted to stop the momentum of team B and allow the home team to regroup. That violates the spirit of the game.

Soccer has no timeouts. The fourth official has no authority to stop the match. Invite the athletic director to sit quietly in the official's area (where the fourth official can keep an eye on the actions) while the senior assistant referee is notified about the weather warning. Assure the athletic director that the information will be relayed to the referee at the next opportunity and that the officials are also interested in the players' safety.

During the pregame, discuss the possibility of a weather suspension because of the inclement weather. How do you determine the need for a stoppage due to lightning? (Less than a 12-second delay between viewing the lightning and hearing the thunder means it is dangerous.) Who should be watching for lightning? (Answer: the fourth official.) How do you notify the referee if that situation developed? (Answer: tell the senior assistant, who flags during a stoppage in play and calls the referee over to relay the information.) According to law 5 (or rule 5 if playing under Federation or NCAA rules), the referee then decides what actions to take. Potential actions are to continue playing, suspend the game until the dangerous weather passes, wait a predetermined amount of time or terminate the match with a written report going to the competition organizer. They will decide whether the game is to be replayed or if the score stands as is, based on the circumstances and time of the game.

The Case of the Guilty Victim

Apparently at halftime, team B discussed how to stop A10. Part of their strategy is a new marker. Another part of the strategy might be for defenders to hold A10 with the hands between the bodies where they can be shielded from the referee's vision. That would frustrate A10 and perhaps draw a card for misconduct.

Change your positioning from outside the players to more behind and inside. Here you can see between the two bodies and catch the holding as A10 tries to go around B3. In any match with sophisticated teams, vary your positioning because players get used to where you will be and they will find your "blind spots."

The Case of Insufficient Information

According to FIFA, when in doubt, do not signal for offside. But you still want to "get it right." Having been burned by an assistant's flag for offside on a throw-in before, I trained myself: if the ball was played by a defender or from a throw-in, I do not look at the assistant. That keeps me from reacting to the flag and then regretting it.

In this case, if A9 touches the ball, the referee should look at the assistant to see if A10 is offside. That is the clue to the assistant that A9 must have played the ball. Signal offside. If B2 or no one played the ball, the referee should not even look at the assistant. That should indicate to the assistant that there was no chance of an offside. Keep the flag down and stay even with the second-to-last defender. The secret here is eye contact before signaling and a thorough pregame discussion.

The Case of the Friendly Foe

That actually happened several years ago in a boys' U-19 match. I found out later that B1 and A9 were next-door neighbors. The lesson learned is to find out more about the two teams before the game begins.

The assignor or assistants could have helped me — but I didn't ask. Mistakenly, I decided to caution both for unsporting behavior and restarted with a dropped ball (which A9 allowed B1 to pick up).

The Case of the Friendly Coach

The coach of team A tried to influence the officials. Some coaches try to do that by manipulation (like the coach of team A) while others may try intimidation. Whether the coach has been successful or not, the coach of team B fears that the opponent has been successful. The officials created an appearance of favoritism.

When the first controversial decision goes against team B, that coach is likely to dissent. Prevent any appearance of partiality by keeping conversations with coaches brief and professional. Be courteous but avoid prolonged discussions. If you do get involved in a long discussion with one coach, do the same with the other to avoid the appearance of bias. Better yet, call both coaches together to discuss the question at hand such as a forecast weather problem, a tricky rule question or a potentially dangerous field situation.

The Case of Touchline Friction

During youth matches, the greatest problems are not the players but the parents. The parents can get extremely emotional and "feed on each other's emotion." That causes a downward spiral to get out of control and ends up in spectator fights and referee assaults. An ounce of prevention here can be worth more than a pound of cure.

The *Laws of the Game* specify that coaching should be only done from the technical area. Most youth leagues define that as the team bench areas, or at least restrict it to their own touchline. When opposing parents are next to each other, cheering for opposite teams, expect problems. Coaching from several different parents tends to be confusing to the players, especially if that coaching is from their touchline but meant for the opponents.

Law 5 empowers the referee to "stop, suspend or terminate the match because of outside interference of any kind." Earlier editions of the laws actually mentioned the spectator.

Follow the guidelines set up by your local league. Whether teams sit opposite the fans or team A sits with team A supporters, all referees working that league should support the same guidelines. If the guidelines are not clear, work with the league to draft workable restrictions. Intermingled spectators invite trouble.

(Dick Arnold, Cheyenne, Wyo., is an elementary school teacher. He is a U.S. Soccer National Referee. He is also a trained assessor and instructor and travels extensively to officiate soccer, including the Dallas Cup.)

Chapter 9

Recognizing Foul Play

By Bob Wertz

Recognizing foul play often draws varied comments from officials. In Louisiana, and generally true for the last 10 years in USSF, one of the top problems that keeps referees from being promoted to State Referee 2 (grade 6) is their inability to recognize fouls.

In deciding whether an incident is foul play or not, you might consider why fouls are committed. Here are eight major reasons most fouls are committed:

1. Challenge for the ball
2. Gain position/prevent an opponent from gaining position
3. Prevent a goal
4. Score a goal
5. Delay the attack
6. Retaliation
7. Intimidation
8. Frustration

Next, consider *where* fouls are generally committed. Let's look at situations and anticipate what's likely to happen:

Set plays

On corner kicks, look for goalkeeper obstruction, holding, pushing and jumping at (crashing into defenders, the goalkeeper, etc., to score a goal). On goalkicks, get to midfield (or where ball is likely to come into play) to look for pushing or holding in the back. On free kicks, look for holding, obstruction and pushing. Referees rarely recognize goalkeeper obstruction, even at the top level.

Breakaways

Look for holding by defenders to delay the attack, pushing by attackers to gain position from the defenders, illegal charges by the defender to throw the attacker off stride, etc. Watch for deliberate handling of the ball to delay the attack.

Outside the penalty area

Look for tackles that are ill timed or poorly executed. Look particularly for the clever player who plays the ball away and then hooks the opponent's ankle to pull the player down. Watch any tripping fouls closely to distinguish fouls in which a defender trips an opponent versus those incidents when an attacker falls over the outstretched legs of an opponent.

Balls in the air

Look for pushing or jumping at an opponent to intimidate the player with no intent to play the ball. (As a hint, the player's head is usually down, with the eyes focused away from the ball and the chin cocked down). I often observe that foul in competitive youth play and notice little or no attempt by the referee to stop it.

Tony Stanley, a USSF national assessor from Memphis, Tenn., has analyzed fouls and foul play for more than 25 years. Based on his analysis, more than 60 percent of all fouls occur within 20 yards of the halfway line. And, more fouls are committed in the second half than the first half. His analysis also shows that the winning team generally commits more fouls. He adds that European background players don't like holding offenses and that South American players abhor heavy tackles.

What is a foul?

As Bob Evans (former FIFA referee, FIFA instructor, USSF national instructor and national director of instruction) declared in the late '80s, referees make decisions about whether a player commits a foul based on what they see that player do. That thought is reinforced in the USSF *Advice to Referees* 12.1.

How to judge an incident

As for evaluating an incident, these criteria are useful. The tips are derived from an article entitled "Intent and How to Judge" by Bob Sumpter, then a USSF national instructor, in *Behind the Whistle* (out of print) in the early l980s.

How can you evaluate if the action was fair or unfair?

• Observe the player's attention. Watch the player's eyes. Is the player playing the ball or the opponent?

• Consider the manner of action or act. Is the player involved in the incident skilled or unskilled? The difference in skill level may be the difference between unsafe play (dangerous) and foul play (some deliberateness or intent). That important distinction affects the punishment the referee administers (indirect free kick versus direct free kick or penalty kick). Skillful players might illegally use an extra move or hip action to counter an opponent.

• Concentrate on the split second before contact. Observe the body actions of both players. Are they part of the play or are they part of a move to unfairly obtain possession of the ball?

• Listen to the sounds made by a player. Listen for grunts or other language that might tip you off to a player's intention.

Finally, Sumpter closed the article with the following guidelines in evaluating an incident:

• Go with your first impression.

• Be consistent judging play. A trip at midfield should be the same as a trip in the penalty area.

• Focus your attention on the sequence of the incident (before, during or after).

Knowing why fouls are committed and where they occur assists you in using techniques to prevent them. Two preventive techniques are helpful for any referee:

Presence

You have to be there and be fit to be there. Your presence discourages players from committing unfair acts. From the A-League to youth play, it's the lack of presence (caused by lack of fitness or ability to read the game) that creates problems. Game control suffers because the players lose respect for the referee. The referee's credibility, in turn, suffers.

Appropriate voice commands

"Hands down," "Back off," and "Lay off the ankles" help seed the proper atmosphere for a safe and well-played game. It's not a question of using the phrases, it's generally a question of referees opening their mouths and setting the tone for the match. Know when the incidents are likely to occur. Learn to read when incidents are simmering and how to pour water, not gasoline, on them.

The information here can be a useful guide for referees to draw the line between fair and unfair play, recognize it for what it is and develop techniques to prevent it. Look for these actions in your games and use the techniques offered by Stanley and Sumpter.

The assessor's role

Imagine you've been sent to observe a referee's performance. The game begins rather uneventfully but soon it becomes obvious that the referee is "letting a lot of things go." Silently, you ponder what effects those no-calls will have. For less-experienced referees, the no-calls lead quickly to a loss of control. For more qualified referees, they can "let 'em play," knowing when the reins have to be pulled — knowing the moment of truth. The dilemma for the assessor is this: Is there a problem and, if so, does the referee recognize it? If there isn't a problem yet, does the referee still recognize the consequences of not acting?

Stanley provides a framework to analyze each incident in a match. First, start with an incident itself. Was it a foul? Yes or no? If yes, then was play stopped? Yes or no? If no, there are several possibilities:

- The referee did not see it
- The referee saw it but did not recognize it
- The referee saw it, but didn't have the courage to call it
- The referee saw it as a trifling foul leading to a no-call
- The referee saw it, determined advantage and called "Play on!"

In my experience, the first bullet relates closely to the referee's positioning, and to a lesser extent, fitness. Did the referee have a poor position to observe an incident and, if so, why? Some possibilities are a bad angle, being screened out by a player, standing in the center circle with play at the far end, staying outside the penalty area and far away from the goal on a corner kick or standing near the player taking a free kick instead of being in an area where the ball is likely to be played toward.

Of the five possibilities, I believe that not recognizing a foul is a referee's biggest problem. The referee looks right at an incident and doesn't recognize the player's actions for what they are. That is an instruction problem, to be addressed by simulated foul demonstrations at recertification clinics. When was the last time you saw that done? Did the instructor cover those fouls seen at the youth level? Did the instructor address a "making a back" foul (player submarining another who is jumping for a header)? Did someone cover an "over the ball" foul, "sandwich" obstruction or a flying elbow on a breakaway (indicates covert holding or pushing)? Did the instructor discuss the dangers of tripping fouls directed at a player's Achilles' tendon instead of the ball? There may be 10 penal fouls listed in the *Laws of the Game* but I suggest that there are a lot more variations of those 10 being committed.

Bullet 3 usually involves a foul that results in a penalty kick. Of course, the penalty kick has its own psychological implications. What are circumstances of the match? Is it a championship match? Is the game televised? Is it a foul in the last minute of a tied or scoreless game? If you believe those things do not influence a referee, then think again.

Trifling fouls generally occur in matches where the players have some skill and referees demonstrate their recognition of that skill. The fewer skilled players on one or both teams, the less likely that the teams consider the fouls trivial. Less-skilled players or teams tend to complain about incidents they believe are fouls, although such incidents tend to be incidental contact and not foul play. So, does the referee act accordingly? Foul play that may seem trivial to an experienced amateur player may not be to a youth recreation player. That is where senior referees who work mostly top-level amateur matches get into trouble with lower-level youth matches. That's also why the youth regional tournaments want State Referees who work a lot of youth matches rather than amateur matches exclusively. On the other side of the coin are top-level players who suddenly become new referees. In my experience, those new referees tend to let everything go for different reasons — not because they don't recognize the foul but because those fouls seem trivial from their playing experience. It's only when they encounter game control problems later in the match that they soon realize there's a problem.

For the skilled referee, the use of advantage is a definite plus to the game. However, what I often observe in youth matches with inexperienced referees is the use of advantage when none existed. There may be an incident that is not a foul but the advantage signal is used anyway. I observe it quite often with grade 7 referees who haven't learned to say, "Continue," "No problem," "Not deliberate," or whatever you are comfortable with to let the players know you observed an incident but are allowing play to continue. I'm not suggesting the use of a one-hand advantage signal that I often observe being incorrectly used for that purpose.

For the referee, as Stanley says, "It is important that in recognizing foul play, you learn to anticipate so that you will know exactly where to look, when to look, know what you are looking for and why." He adds, "Your responsibility is to know where the danger areas are located and which of the two teams will likely commit the preponderance of fouls or infractions."

(Bob Wertz is a former chair of the USSF referee committee and chairs the Louisiana state referee committee. Wertz lives in Baton Rouge, La., and is a state instructor, state assessor and an emeritus State Referee and serves as a liaison to the Louisiana High School Athletic Association.)

NOTES

NOTES

NOTES

NOTES

NOTES

NOTES

NOTES

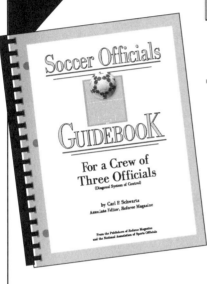

Thinking Soccer: Officiating Success Techniques

Your complete guide to soccer officiating philosophy and hands-on techniques to enhance your performance! Page after page of important information and innovations on how to stay focused, stay in control and have more fun working the game you love! Included:

• Techniques and philosophies of officiating the diagonal and dual systems of control
• Restarts: Throw-ins, goal kicks, corner kicks, free kicks, drop balls
• Communication techniques
• Dealing with dissent
• Appearance and professionalism
• Getting in shape and staying healthy

6" x 9" paperback, 87 pages.

Order Code:	BTS
Regular Price:	$12.95
NASO-Member Price:	$10.35

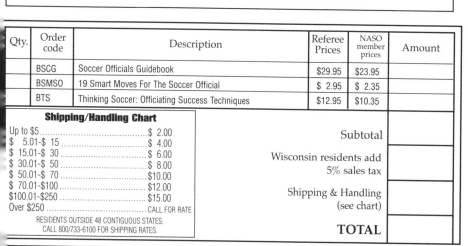

Qty.	Order code	Description	Referee Prices	NASO member prices	Amount
	BSCG	Soccer Officials Guidebook	$29.95	$23.95	
	BSMSO	19 Smart Moves For The Soccer Official	$ 2.95	$ 2.35	
	BTS	Thinking Soccer: Officiating Success Techniques	$12.95	$10.35	

Shipping/Handling Chart

Up to $5	$ 2.00
$ 5.01-$ 15	$ 4.00
$ 15.01-$ 30	$ 6.00
$ 30.01-$ 50	$ 8.00
$ 50.01-$ 70	$10.00
$ 70.01-$100	$12.00
$100.01-$250	$15.00
Over $250	CALL FOR RATE

RESIDENTS OUTSIDE 48 CONTIGUOUS STATES:
CALL 800/733-6100 FOR SHIPPING RATES.

Subtotal

Wisconsin residents add
5% sales tax

Shipping & Handling
(see chart)

TOTAL

Name_____ Address_____

City, State, Zip_____ Daytime Phone_____

Referee/NASO Account #_____

❑ Check/Money order   ❑ MasterCard   ❑ VISA

Account #_____ Expiration Date _____

Signature_____
(required only if using credit card)

S099

ORDERING MADE EASY!
Call toll-free
800/733-6100
and use your Visa or MasterCard!

IF YOU

LIKE THIS

The only magazine exclusively for sports officials

Rulings, caseplays, mechanics – in-depth

BOOK,

Solid coverage of the sport(s) you work

YOU'LL

Important, late-breaking news stories

LOVE

Thought-provoking interviews and features

THIS MAGAZINE!

Opinions/editorials on vital topics